A BiG BOOK OF SMALL iDEAS

50 CREATiONS By NENDO

A BiG BOOK OF SMALL iDEAS

50 CREATiONS By NENDO

OKi SATO

with

GENEViÈVE GALLOT

T&H

ABOUT THIS BOOK

OKI SATO
NENDO

THERE ARE MANY BEAUTIFULLY MADE DESIGN BOOKS AND ART BOOKS WITH PHOTOGRAPHS AND TEXTS. I HAVE BEEN FORTUNATE TO HAVE PUBLISHED SUCH BOOKS IN THE PAST, AND WHILE THEY ARE GREAT FOR UNDERSTANDING THE WORK ITSELF, IT ISN'T EASY TO DECIPHER THE STORY BEHIND THE WORK. DESIGN IS NOT ONLY ABOUT SURFACE-LEVEL ELEMENTS SUCH AS SHAPES, COLOURS AND FINISHES. ITS CORE VALUE LIES IN THE CONCEPT THAT DRIVES THESE ELEMENTS. ARTICULATING THIS HAS BEEN A LIFELONG EXPLORATION OF MINE.

THIS BOOK WAS CREATED WITH THESE CHALLENGES IN MIND AND EVOLVED INTO A RATHER CURIOUS JUMBLE OF PHOTOGRAPHS, SKETCHES AND TEXTS. IT RECREATES THE VIEW SEEN OVER MY DESK WHEN WORKING ON A CONCEPT. TO ACHIEVE THIS, PRODUCT PHOTOGRAPHS ARE PRESENTED AT FULL SCALE WHEREVER POSSIBLE, AVOIDING MULTIPLE ANGLES ON THE SAME PAGE. THAT IS WHY THIS TURNED OUT TO BE A BOOK OF CONSIDERABLE SIZE.

THE STARTING POINT OF A PROJECT CAN BE ANYTHING FROM A LOGICAL ANALYSIS OF A MECHANISM TO AN ABSTRACT, INTUITIVE IDEA. IT CAN THEN BEGIN TO FLOW IN ONE DIRECTION, DIVERGE, DIGRESS, RECONNECT, EBBING AND FLOWING. SKETCHES AND TEXTS ARE SIMILARLY SCATTERED THROUGHOUT THIS BOOK.

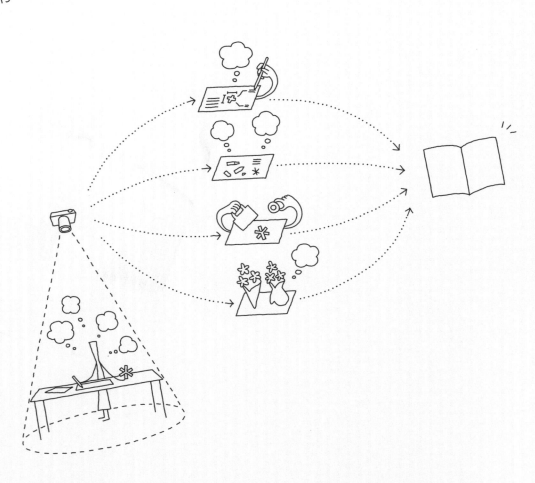

OUR STUDIO HAS WORKED ON OVER A FEW THOUSAND PROJECTS THAT RANGE
FROM INTERIORS AND ARCHITECTURE, FURNITURE AND PRODUCT DESIGN,
GRAPHIC DESIGN INCLUDING LOGOS AND PACKAGING, TO ART INSTALLATIONS
FOR MUSEUMS AND GALLERIES. THE WORKS SELECTED FOR THIS BOOK ARE
ALL 'SMALL IDEAS' THAT CREATE 'FUNCTIONAL VALUE' IN PARTICULAR. LIKE
PROVIDING A PLACE TO SET DOWN A SPOON, OR SMALL ADJUSTMENTS THAT
MAKE TURNING A DOOR KEY EASIER. THE POWER OF THESE IDEAS IS MINIMAL;
IT BRINGS AN ELEMENT OF JOY AND SURPRISE TO OUR DAILY LIVES AND IS
VERY NEAR AND DEAR TO MY HEART.

IN ADDITION, THE BOOK FEATURES PROJECTS THAT ADDRESS CONTEMPORARY
SOCIAL ISSUES: BRINGING THE FUN OF PLAYING FOOTBALL TO CHILDREN IN
NEED, PROVIDING SUPPORT TO STRUGGLING FARMERS DEALING WITH FOOD
WASTE, OR CREATING ECO-FRIENDLY PACKAGING THAT REDUCES ENVIRONMENTAL
IMPACT. WE HAVE ALSO INCLUDED DESIGNS THAT UTILIZE THE SENSES IN A
VARIETY OF WAYS, SUCH AS CHOCOLATES IN A RANGE OF SHAPES THAT SEEM
TO TASTE DIFFERENT, OR CONTAINERS THAT MAKE DIFFERENT SOUNDS TO
REFLECT THEIR CONTENTS.

WE HOPE THAT THIS BOOK WILL HELP READERS TO REALIZE THAT INFINITE
POSSIBILITIES FOR NEW IDEAS EXIST IN EVERYDAY ITEMS, COMMONLY FOUND
AROUND US, FROM A PAPER CLIP TO A SKIPPING ROPE OR A ZIPPER. BY
FOCUSING ON THE ORDINARY RATHER THAN THE EXTRAORDINARY, WE CAN
ADD A PINCH OF COLOUR TO OUR DAILY LIVES. INSTEAD OF EXAMINING THE
SURFACE-LEVEL ASPECTS OF A COMPLETED WORK, WE WANT ITS UNDERLYING
INTRINSIC NATURE TO BE RECOGNIZED.

WE HOPE THAT THIS WILL HELP THE SEEDS OF 'SMALL IDEAS' TO SPROUT
INSIDE ALL OF YOU ONE DAY.

NENDO ☺.

'WITH DESIGN, YOU HAVE TO MAKE PEOPLE HAPPY — FUN + FUNCTION'

GENEVIÈVE GALLOT

BORN IN 1977 IN TORONTO, CANADA, OKI SATO ARRIVED IN TOKYO AT THE AGE OF TEN. HE GRADUATED AS AN ARCHITECT FROM WASEDA UNIVERSITY IN TOKYO IN 2002. THE SAME YEAR, HE WENT ON A STUDY TRIP TO THE SALONE DEL MOBILE IN MILAN, WHERE HE WAS IMPRESSED BY THE FREEDOM THAT REIGNED THERE, AND FOUNDED HIS STUDIO NENDO, A TERM THAT MEANS 'MODELLING CLAY' IN JAPANESE.

IN 2005, HE OPENED A SECOND OFFICE IN MILAN, A CITY THAT REMAINS A CONTINUING SOURCE OF INSPIRATION FOR HIM. RANKED BY NEWSWEEK MAGAZINE AMONG THE '100 MOST RESPECTED JAPANESE PEOPLE' IN 2006, HE HAS RECEIVED NUMEROUS AWARDS, NOTABLY DESIGNER OF THE YEAR AWARDS FROM WALLPAPER* AND ELLE DECO MAGAZINES IN 2012, FROM THE TRADE FAIR MAISON ET OBJET IN 2015, AND FROM THE MAGAZINE AW ARCHITEKTUR & WOHNEN IN 2019. HIS CREATIONS CAN BE SEEN ALL OVER THE WORLD AND IN THE COLLECTIONS OF MANY INTERNATIONAL MUSEUMS (MOMA IN NEW YORK, THE MUSÉE DES ARTS DÉCORATIFS AND CENTRE POMPIDOU IN PARIS, THE V&A IN LONDON, THE MUSÉE DES BEAUX-ARTS IN MONTRÉAL, THE TRIENNALE DI MILANO, 21_21 DESIGN SIGHT IN TOKYO, AND MORE). HIS OBJECTS ARE MANUFACTURED BY NUMEROUS BRANDS (CAPPELLINI, MOROSO, EMECO, ETC.).

IN TOKYO, HIS STUDIO IS LOCATED IN A BUILDING CREATED BY KENZO TANGE, WITH A STONE GARDEN DESIGNED BY ISAMU NOGUCHI AND A CAFÉ MANAGED BY NENDO. ITS OUTPUT IS CONSIDERABLE AND ITS CREATIVE SCOPE UNLIMITED WITHIN THE REALM OF ARCHITECTURE AND DESIGN, RANGING FROM SHOPPING MALLS (SIAM DISCOVERY IN BANGKOK, 40,000M²), EXHIBITIONS, BOOKS, GRAPHICS, FURNITURE, INTERIOR SPACES AND OBJECTS, DOWN TO PAPER CLIPS AND BEER CANS. SINCE THE CREATION OF NENDO, OKI SATO HAS COMBINED MANY DIFFERENT SCALES IN HIS WORK. BUT, FOR HIM, THE BASIC APPROACH IS THE SAME FOR BOTH PAPER CLIPS AND LARGE COMMERCIAL FACILITIES, EVEN THOUGH THE FORM AND SCALE OF THE OUTPUT ARE DIFFERENT. OKI BELIEVES THAT THE PEOPLE WHO USE PAPER CLIPS AND THE PEOPLE WHO USE LARGE COMMERCIAL FACILITIES ARE THE SAME PEOPLE. THAT'S WHY EVERY PROJECT STARTS BY FOCUSING ON HOW PEOPLE REACT, FEEL AND ACT. OKI CALLS THIS SEQUENCE OF EVENTS A 'STORY', AND CALLS HIMSELF PRIMARILY A 'STORYTELLER'.

WHEN OKI FIRST DISCOVERED TOKYO, IT WAS A CULTURE SHOCK. THE PLACE WHERE HE GREW UP IN CANADA WAS VERY RURAL. HIS NEW DAILY LIFE IN JAPAN SEEMED FANTASTICAL TO HIM AND ENCOURAGED HIM TO PAY ATTENTION TO THE MOST ORDINARY DETAILS. AS A DESIGNER, HE BEGINS BY WORKING WITH SKETCHES — HE CONSIDERS HIMSELF A POOR DRAUGHTSMAN — AND QUICKLY MOVES ON TO 3D PRINTERS. FOR HIM, IT IS ESSENTIAL NOT TO GET STUCK ON HIS EARLY IDEAS. HE LIKES TO LET AN IDEA GO SO THAT A NEW IDEA ARISES. 'IT'S LIKE BREATHING, IN AND OUT,' HE SAYS. OKI SATO EXUDES DESIGN 24 HOURS A DAY, OR ALMOST. AS FOR THE REST, HE HAS FORTY WHITE SHIRTS THAT HE ORDERS ONLINE FROM UNIQLO, AND TEN PAIRS OF THE SAME BLACK ADIDAS STAN SMITHS, TO REMOVE THE NEED FOR SHOPPING. PLUS A FAITHFUL COMPANION ALWAYS BY HIS SIDE: HIS DOG KINAKO, HALF-PUG, HALF-CHIHUAHUA.

IN 2007, WHEN THE FASHION DESIGNER ISSEY MIYAKE ASKED HIM TO DESIGN A CHAIR, OKI SATO THOUGHT OF THE MOUNDS OF PAPER THAT THE COMPANY USED TO THROW AWAY AS A BYPRODUCT OF THEIR FAMOUS PLEATS PLEASE RANGE, AND USED THEM TO CREATE THE CABBAGE CHAIR. ONCE THE SHEETS OF PAPER WERE ROLLED INTO A THICK SHEAF, OKI BEGAN TO 'PEEL' THEM BACK. AT ONE POINT, ISSEY TOLD HIM TO STOP: THE CHAIR SEEMED PERFECT TO HIM. 'I WANTED TO CONTINUE,' SAYS OKI. 'BUT ISSEY WAS RIGHT. HE KNEW HOW TO WORK FREELY. MANY DIRECTIONS AND SOLUTIONS ARE POSSIBLE. THAT DESIGN DOES NOT HAVE A SINGLE GOAL. I LEARNED A LOT FROM HIM.' OKI SATO UNDERSTANDS

WITH HIS JAPANESE CULTURE, OKI IS VERY SENSITIVE TO INVISIBLE ELEMENTS SUCH AS THE PASSAGE OF TIME, EMOTIONS, MEMORIES, AND WANTS TO TRANSLATE THEM INTO HIS CREATIONS, IN AN INVENTIVE WAY. THIS IS ALSO WHY HE LOVES THE JAPANESE MANGA SERIES DORAEMON, EVEN THOUGH DORAEMON IS A ROBOT: 'IN EACH STORY, THE MAIN CHARACTER FINDS HIMSELF AT A DEAD END AND, EVERY TIME, SOME SORT OF GADGET COMES TO HIS RESCUE!' HIS WORK CONTAINS REFERENCES TO ORIGAMI, RAKU, TORII AND MANGA, AS WELL AS TO WESTERN WAYS OF LIVING.

HE CREATES A MINIMALIST FORM OF DESIGN, WITH PURE LINES, IMBUED WITH POETRY, HUMOUR, SURPRISE AND SUBTLETY. HE ALSO WANTS IT TO BE USER-FRIENDLY, EASILY FORMING CONNECTIONS BETWEEN HUMANS AND THE SPACE OR PRODUCT. HIS OBJECTS ARE SIMPLE, INGENIOUS, OFTEN INTRIGUING, EVEN UNEXPECTED. AND, ALTHOUGH THE BORDER BETWEEN ART AND DESIGN SOMETIMES SEEMS TENUOUS TO HIM, OKI SATO, LIKE ISSEY MIYAKE, BELIEVES IN THIS DIFFERENCE: WITH ART, YOU CAN MAKE PEOPLE SAD, BUT WITH DESIGN, YOU MUST MAKE THEM HAPPY. OKI'S DESIRE IS TO HELP CREATE A WORLD OF HARMONY AND BALANCE. THAT'S WHY HE SOMETIMES INCORPORATES HUMOUR OR 'SPICE' INTO HIS DESIGNS TO MAKE THEM FRIENDLIER. 'GOOD DESIGN IS FUNCTIONAL, SIMPLE AND USER-FRIENDLY. FUN + FUNCTION.' 'FUN' IS PART OF THE WORD 'FUNCTION', AND THE SELECTION OF WORKS IN THIS BOOK IS THE VERY EMBODIMENT OF THE 'FUN + FUNCTION' PRINCIPLE.

OKI FEELS THAT DESIGN HAS TO 'SOLVE A PROBLEM' OF SOME SORT. IT CAN BE A TRIVIAL OR LATENT ISSUE THAT NO ONE CARES ABOUT. THERE ARE ALSO CASES THAT HAVE A VERY GRADUAL YET LONG-LASTING IMPACT ON THE ISSUE. SOME SEEM LIKE WORKS OF ART AT FIRST GLANCE BUT ULTIMATELY ARE ALSO DESIGNS. OKI SATO POINTS OUT THAT THE CONTINENTS MOVE SEVERAL CENTIMETRES A YEAR DUE TO TECTONIC MOTION: 'I FEEL THAT THE ACCUMULATION OF PROBLEM-SOLVING THROUGH DESIGN IS LIKE THAT MOTION: DESIGN CREATES A SUBTLE, SLOW, POSITIVE IMPACT ON SOCIETY. IT MAY BE DIFFICULT TO IMAGINE THAT A SINGLE DESIGN WILL COMPLETELY CHANGE SOCIETY BUT THAT DOES NOT MEAN THAT I AM PESSIMISTIC ABOUT THE POWER OF DESIGN.'

OKI SATO LIKES TO HAVE SMALL EVERYDAY ROUTINES – CAPPUCCINO IN THE MORNING, A WALK WITH HIS DOG – AND TRIES TO FOCUS ON THE SMALL THINGS AS MUCH AS POSSIBLE. SMALL DIFFERENCES. SMALL SIMILARITIES. SMALL PROBLEMS. SMALL JOYS. THESE THINGS ARE ALWAYS THE STARTING POINT. 'THE DESIGN LOOKS AS IF MULTIPLE ELEMENTS – THE RIGHT MATERIALS, SHAPES, FUNCTIONS, STRUCTURES, MANUFACTURING METHODS – ARE PIECED TOGETHER ONE AT A TIME, LIKE A PUZZLE. IT IS NOT A BIG IDEA AT THE BEGINNING. IT IS RATHER LIKE TAKING A SMALL IDEA AND DEVELOPING IT INTO A BIG IDEA.'

WORKING ON BOUNDARIES, THE DESIGNER WANTS TO COMBINE A RESPECT FOR CERTAIN RULES AND THE VITAL FREEDOM OF CREATION. FOR HIM, REGULATIONS AND CONSTRAINTS MAKE IT EASIER TO GENERATE IDEAS. THE WORST PROJECT WOULD BE THE ONE WITH NO SPECIFIC REQUESTS, THE DEMAND TO CREATE SOMETHING 'FREE'. 'I ALWAYS TRY TO BE AWARE OF THE BOUNDARIES OF THINGS. WHAT ARE CHOPSTICKS? THEY'RE A KIND OF TABLEWARE THAT ALLOWS YOU TO EAT BY USING TWO STICKS. BUT CHOPSTICKS REALLY CAN'T BE CHOPSTICKS UNLESS THERE ARE TWO OF THEM. THE STARTING POINT IS TO FEEL THE "WAVERING OF THE BOUNDARY" WITHIN THE OBJECT AND THIS LEADS TO THE DESIGN OF A SINGLE SPIRAL-SHAPED CHOPSTICK THAT SOLVES THE PROBLEM OF CARRYING THE DOUBLE ITEM.'

OKi SATO'S WORK iS OFTEN SHOWN iN MUSEUMS AND GALLERiES AROUND THE WORLD (MiLAN TRiENNALE, DESiGN MUSEUM HOLON, ViCTORiA & ALBERT MUSEUM). HE ALSO DESiGNS LARGE-SCALE iNSTALLATiONS THAT OFFER 'EXPERiENCES' (BON MARCHÉ, PARiS) AND SOMETiMES PRODUCES 'OBJECT SYSTEMS' RATHER THAN OBJECTS ALONE. THE WAYS TO MAKE PEOPLE SMiLE ARE MANY AND VARiED. 'NONE OF US HAVE THE SAME PERSONALiTY AND EACH OF US iS UNiQUE. THERE iS NO LiMiT TO THE TYPES OF EMOTiONS AND FEELiNGS THAT DESiGN CAN CREATE. AND JUST AS OUR DAiLY LiVES ARE COLOURED BY A VARiETY OF EMOTiONS, THE EMOTiONAL VALUE OF DESiGN HAS AN iMPORTANT ROLE TO PLAY iN OUR DAiLY LiVES.'

iN 2019, OKi SATO DESiGNED THE N02 RECYCLE CHAiR, MADE FROM PLASTiC HOUSEHOLD WASTE, AND HiS RECENT CREATiONS TAKE GREATER ACCOUNT OF THE MAiN CHALLENGES OF OUR TiME: CLiMATE, ENERGY, ENViRONMENT, POVERTY. OKi iNSiSTS: 'TODAY, THE MOST iMPORTANT THiNG iS THE END OF THE PRODUCT. MANY OF THE MASS-PRODUCED OBJECTS WE ARE CURRENTLY WORKiNG ON ARE MADE USiNG MATERiALS AND CONSTRUCTiON METHODS WiTH LOW ENViRONMENTAL iMPACT. i EXPECT THAT THiS WiLL BECOME THE NORM iN THE NEXT DECADE OR SO.' CURRENTLY NENDO iS WORKiNG ON THE OVERALL DESiGN OF THE JAPAN PAViLiON FOR EXPO 2025 iN OSAKA, JAPAN. FOR THiS PROJECT, LAMiNATED WOOD MADE FROM THiNNED FORESTS WiLL BE USED AND THE CONSTRUCTiON METHOD iS PLANNED SO THAT THE MATERiALS CAN BE REUSED iN OTHER BUiLDiNGS AFTER DiSMANTLiNG. BUT BEYOND HiS AWARENESS OF THE DEMANDS OF THE CURRENT AGE, OKi'S CREATiONS ARE ABOVE ALL A TiMELESS STORY.

FOR 'NENDO SEES KYOTO' iN 2022, OKi SATO DESiGNED A SERiES OF EXCEPTiONAL PiECES iN COLLABORATiON WiTH REMARKABLE LOCAL ARTiSANS. THiS PROJECT WAS A CHANCE TO CELEBRATE TRADiTiONAL CRAFT SKiLLS AND TO REViTALiZE THEM iN A MODERN SPiRiT. OKi iS USUALLY CAREFUL NOT TO TREAT EiTHER TRADiTiONAL OR CUTTiNG-EDGE TECHNOLOGiES AS SPECiAL. 'iF WE WORSHiP TRADiTiONAL TECHNOLOGY TOO MUCH, iT COULD LEAD TO NOSTALGiC DESiGNS OR CONSERVATiVE THiNKiNG, WHiCH iS A RiSK. AND iF WE GET TOO CAUGHT UP iN ADVANCED TECHNOLOGY, WE WiLL BE BLiNDED BY iTS MAGiC AND LOSE SiGHT OF THE ESSENTiAL iSSUES. AS A DESiGNER, i ALWAYS FEEL iT iS iMPORTANT TO ViEW BOTH SPECiAL AND ORDiNARY THiNGS AS FLAT ENTiTiES.'

FOR OKi, PERFECTiON iS BORiNG. iN FACT, HE THiNKS THERE ARE TWO REALiTiES: ONE 'NOTiONAL', THE OTHER 'PHYSiCAL'. 'iF ONE THiNKS OF THE "NOTiON", OF SOMETHiNG THAT LOOKS LiKE A CHAiR OR SMELLS LiKE A CHAiR, THEN THE MiND EXPANDS... GOOD DESiGN iS SOMETHiNG YOU CAN EXPLAiN TO A CHiLD. WHEN DESiGN iS SiMPLE, iT BECOMES GLOBAL. iT GiVES YOU SOLUTiONS AND MAKES YOU SMiLE'. BUT DESiGN iS NEVER FiNiSHED... FOR OKi, THE MOST iNTERESTiNG THiNGS iN LiFE ARE THOSE THAT ARE STiLL UNFiNiSHED. THE ESSENTiAL iS ALWAYS WHAT HASN'T BEEN CREATED YET. 'iT'S PRECiSELY BECAUSE i CANNOT SEE CLEARLY THE FUTURE OF DESiGN THAT i FEEL DESiGN iS ENDLESSLY iNTERESTiNG AND WORTH DEVOTiNG MY ENTiRE LiFE TO.'

FiNALLY, iF YOU ASK OKi SATO WHAT WOULD BE HiS DREAM PROJECT, HE ANSWERS: 'iT WOULD BE A LiTTLE iDEA FOR MYSELF. i'VE BEEN DESiGNiNG FOR OVER TWENTY YEARS AND NEVER DESiGNED FOR MYSELF. BUT i DON'T THiNK iT WiLL HAPPEN TOMORROW...'

THE 50 CREATIONS IN THIS BOOK COME FROM A WIDE VARIETY OVER SEVERAL YEARS UP TO NENDO'S
LATEST MAJOR PROJECT, THE TGV OF THE FUTURE, EXPECTED IN FRANCE IN 2025. OFTEN PLAYFUL, SOME
OF THE OBJECTS WEAVE UNIQUE LINKS BETWEEN OUR DIFFERENT SENSES. CHOCOLATES WITH DIFFERENT
TEXTURES AND TASTES. CANDLES WITH CHANGING COLOURS AND SCENTS. PORCELAIN CONTAINERS THAT
PRODUCE DIVERSE CRYSTALLINE SOUNDS. SOME OBJECTS ARE DESIGNED TO MAKE EVERYDAY LIFE EASIER,
FOR OURSELVES (UMBRELLA, BAG, PAPER CLIPS) OR FOR OUR DOG. OTHERS ARE INTENDED TO SAVE LIVES
IN DANGEROUS SITUATIONS (MINIM+AID) OR TO FULFIL A SPECIFIC NEED (FOOTBALL KIT, PETIT MARKET).
SOME PROJECTS ARE CONNECTED WITH FOOD (PEPPER GRINDER, CANDY CASE), OTHERS TO OKI'S JAPANESE
IDENTITY (BUDDHIST ALTAR) WHILE SEVERAL ARE A SYNTHESIS OF HIS DUAL CULTURES (TROPHIES AND
MEDALS FOR UNIVAS).

IN 2024 NENDO IS WORKING ON 200 PROJECTS ON A DAILY BASIS WITH A TEAM OF ABOUT 60 PEOPLE.

TABLE OF CONTENTS
50 CREATIONS BY NENDO

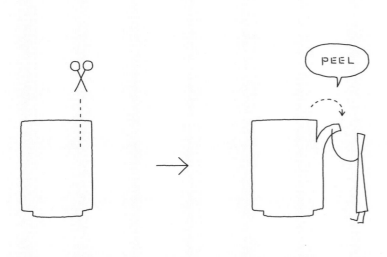

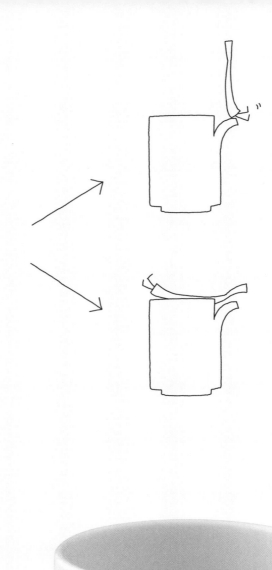

A SMALL SECTION OF RIM OF THIS TEA CUP HAS BEEN 'PEELED' BACK. THIS ALLOWS A TEABAG STRING TO ESCAPE, AND/OR A SPOON TO REMAIN INSIDE WHEN THE USER DRINKS THE TEA OR PUTS ON THE LID IN ORDER TO CARRY IT. THE LID HELPS TO STEEP THE TEA, BUT CAN ALSO BE USED AS A SMALL DISH FOR SWEETS OR BISCUITS, OR TO REST A USED TEABAG OR SPOON ON. THE BASES OF THE CUP AND LID ARE INDENTED FOR EASY STACKING AND STORAGE.

LID　　　　COASTER　　　　SMALL DISH

FASTEN THE TEABAG STRING

REST THE SPOON OR STIRRER

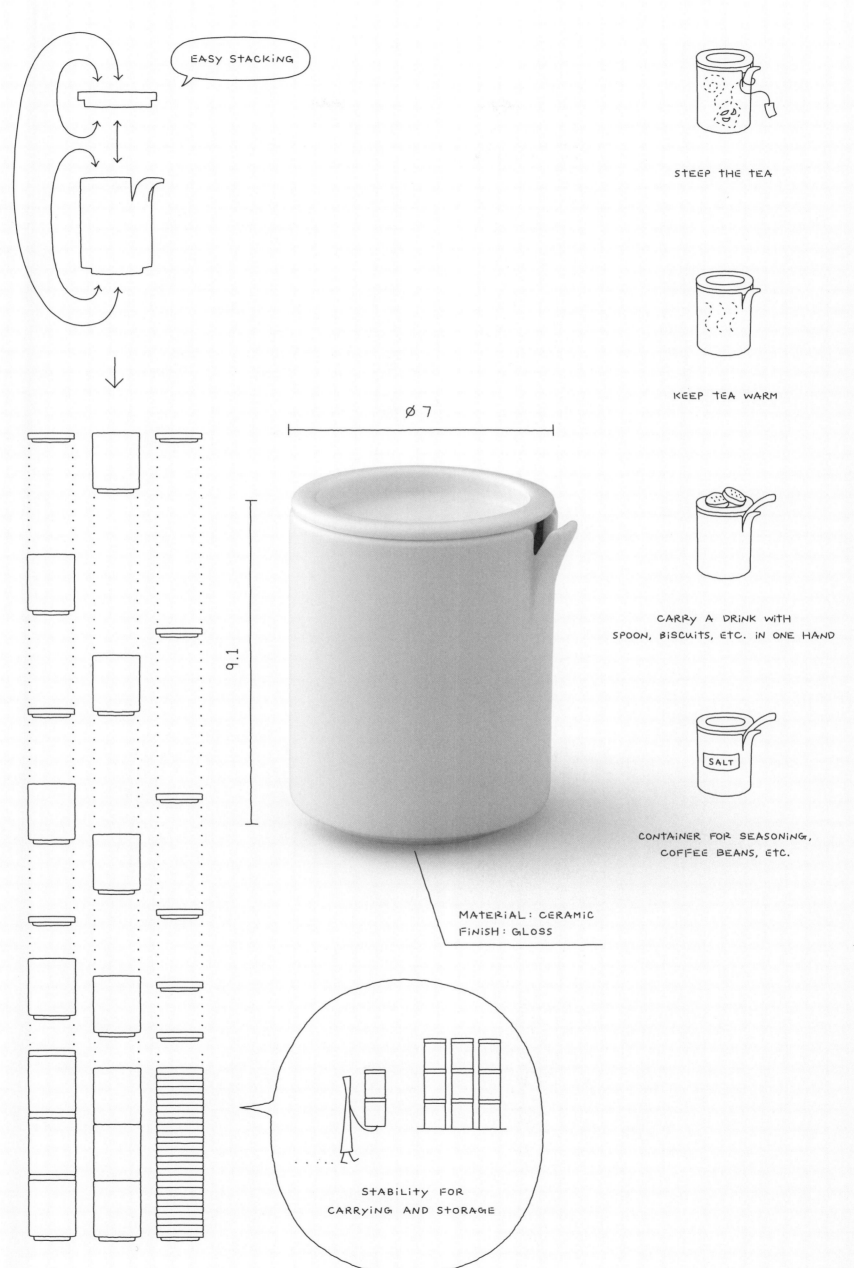

EASY STACKING

Ø 7

9.1

MATERIAL: CERAMIC
FINISH: GLOSS

STEEP THE TEA

KEEP TEA WARM

CARRY A DRINK WITH
SPOON, BISCUITS, ETC. IN ONE HAND

SALT

CONTAINER FOR SEASONING,
COFFEE BEANS, ETC.

STABILITY FOR
CARRYING AND STORAGE

CHOPSTICKS ORDINARILY COME IN PAIRS, BUT THESE CHOPSTICKS ARE A SINGLE UNIT.
THEY CAN BE SEPARATED INTO TWO FOR EATING, THEN REJOINED INTO ONE FORM WHEN NOT IN USE.

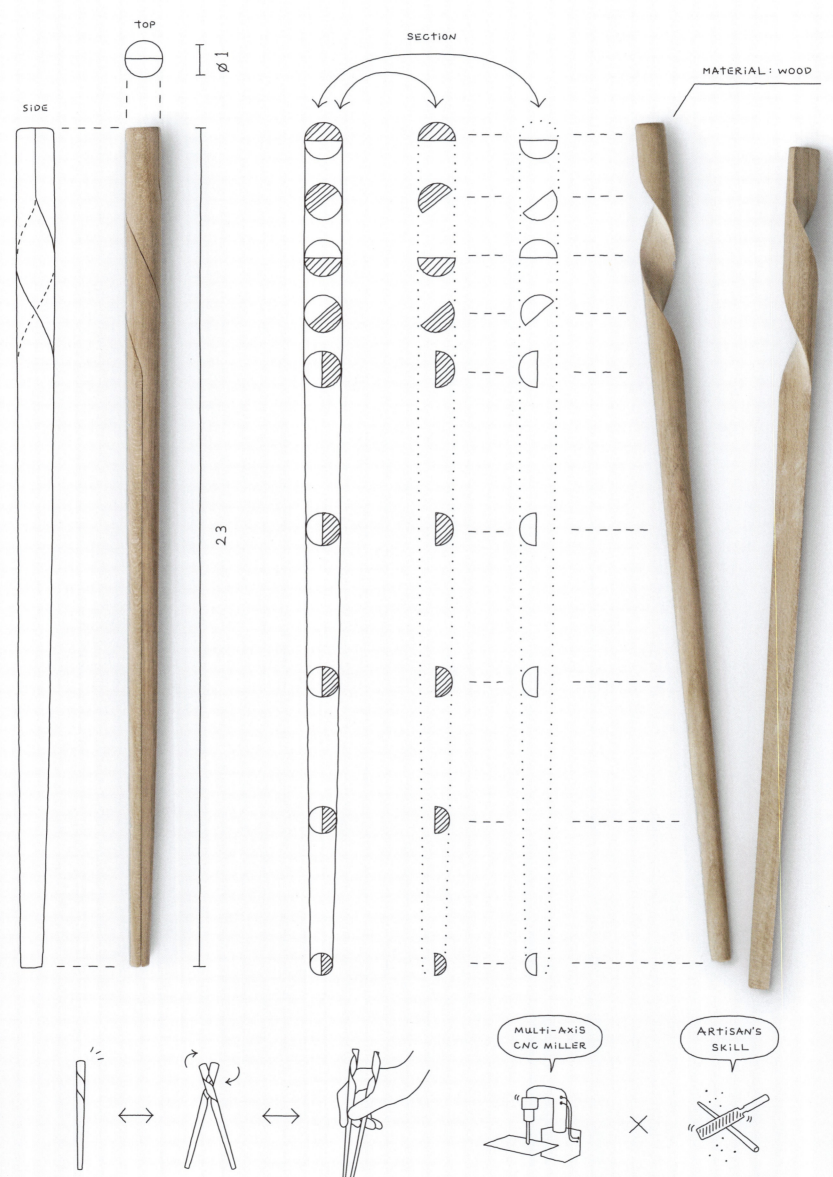

TOP

Ø1

SIDE

SECTION

MATERIAL: WOOD

23

MULTI-AXIS
CNC MILLER

ARTISAN'S
SKILL

MIXING TRADITIONAL AND NEW TECHNOLOGY

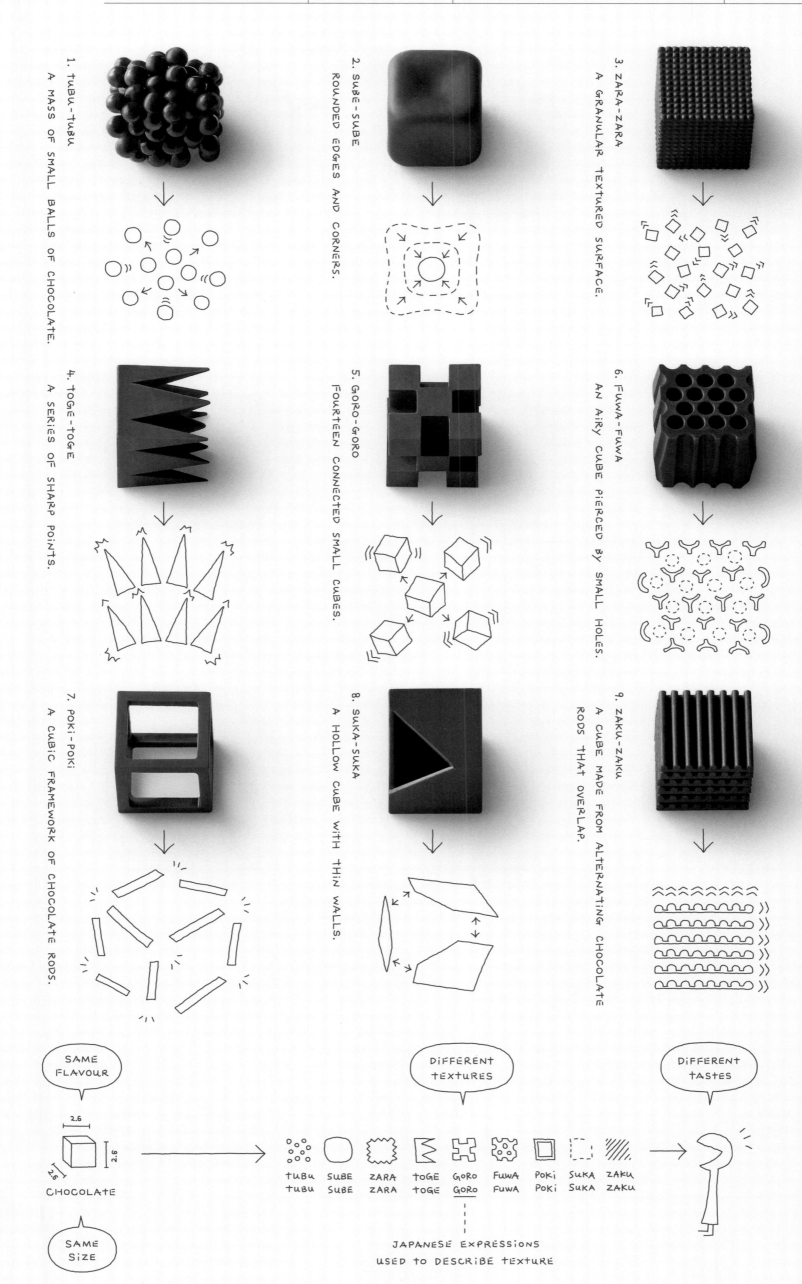

1. TUBU-TUBU
A MASS OF SMALL BALLS OF CHOCOLATE.

2. SUBE-SUBE
ROUNDED EDGES AND CORNERS.

3. ZARA-ZARA
A GRANULAR TEXTURED SURFACE.

4. TOGE-TOGE
A SERIES OF SHARP POINTS.

5. GORO-GORO
FOURTEEN CONNECTED SMALL CUBES.

6. FUWA-FUWA
AN AIRY CUBE PIERCED BY SMALL HOLES.

7. POKI-POKI
A CUBIC FRAMEWORK OF CHOCOLATE RODS.

8. SUKA-SUKA
A HOLLOW CUBE WITH THIN WALLS.

9. ZAKU-ZAKU
A CUBE MADE FROM ALTERNATING CHOCOLATE RODS THAT OVERLAP.

SAME FLAVOUR

DIFFERENT TEXTURES

DIFFERENT TASTES

2.6
2.6
2.6
CHOCOLATE

SAME SIZE

TUBU TUBU | SUBE SUBE | ZARA ZARA | TOGE TOGE | GORO GORO | FUWA FUWA | POKI POKI | SUKA SUKA | ZAKU ZAKU

JAPANESE EXPRESSIONS
USED TO DESCRIBE TEXTURE

HOUSE

WATER BOWL

TOY

40
Ø 60
20

THE HOUSE BECOMES A LITTLE CAVE WHEN DOGS CURL UP INSIDE IT, AND A BED WHEN THEY LIE ON TOP.

HOUSE

WATER

BONE

MATERIAL: SILICON RUBBER

Ø 9
15

THE BONE CAN BE TRANSFORMED INTO A BALL BY FOLDING IN THE TWO ENDS.

A THREE-PIECE COLLECTION OF DOG ACCESSORIES, CONSISTING OF A HOUSE, A BOWL AND A TOY.
AS A RESULT OF SEEKING FORMS THAT COULD CREATE STABILITY IN DIFFERENT SHAPES, THE
COLLECTION IS MADE FROM TRIANGULAR PANELS FORMING A POLYGON MESH.

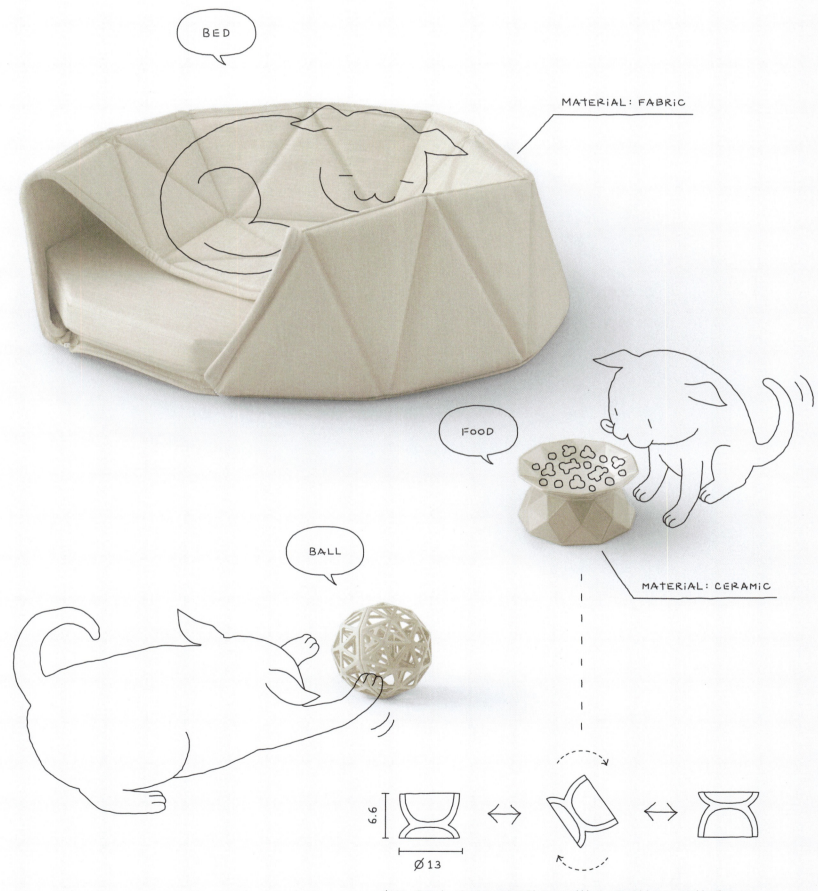

BED

MATERIAL: FABRIC

FOOD

MATERIAL: CERAMIC

BALL

9.9

Ø 13

THE BOWL IS REVERSIBLE, WITH A SHALLOW DISH FOR FOOD
ON ONE SIDE AND A DEEPER DISH FOR WATER ON THE OTHER.

| Project: CUBIC RUBBER-BAND | Item: RUBBER BAND | Client: By│N | Year: 2014 |
| Project: LINK CLIP | Item: PAPER CLIP | Client: By│N | Year: 2014 |

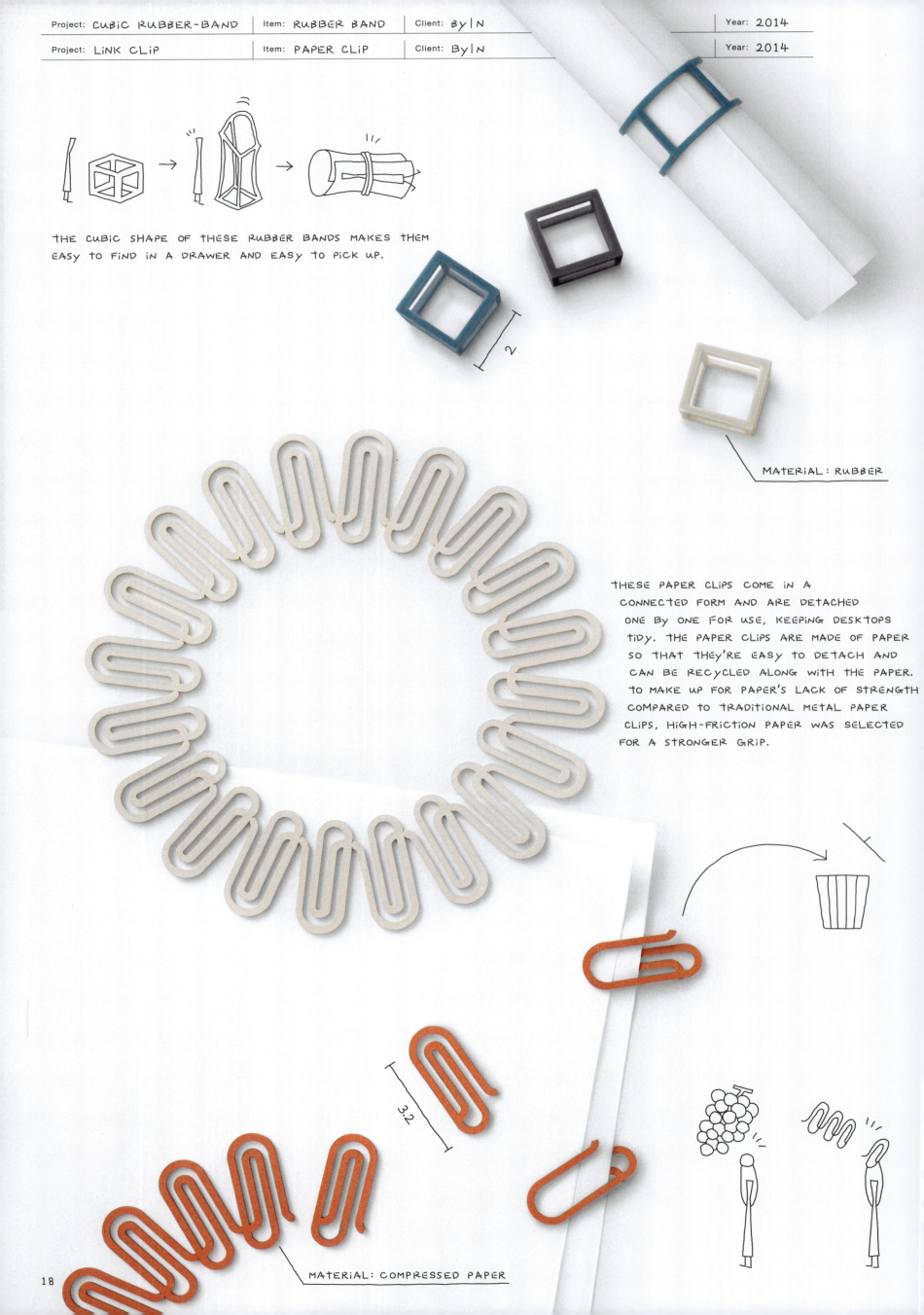

THE CUBIC SHAPE OF THESE RUBBER BANDS MAKES THEM
EASY TO FIND IN A DRAWER AND EASY TO PICK UP.

MATERIAL: RUBBER

THESE PAPER CLIPS COME IN A
CONNECTED FORM AND ARE DETACHED
ONE BY ONE FOR USE, KEEPING DESKTOPS
TIDY. THE PAPER CLIPS ARE MADE OF PAPER
SO THAT THEY'RE EASY TO DETACH AND
CAN BE RECYCLED ALONG WITH THE PAPER.
TO MAKE UP FOR PAPER'S LACK OF STRENGTH
COMPARED TO TRADITIONAL METAL PAPER
CLIPS, HIGH-FRICTION PAPER WAS SELECTED
FOR A STRONGER GRIP.

MATERIAL: COMPRESSED PAPER

WHITE

GRADATION

BLACK

A CLEAR
ACRYLIC RULER
WITH MARKINGS THAT
GRADATE FROM WHITE TO BLACK,
MAKING THE RULER EASY TO USE
ON BOTH DARK AND LIGHT SURFACES.

MATERIAL: ACRYLIC

FLAT & WIDE OBJECTS
· NOTEPAPER
· CARD
· RULER

TALL OBJECTS
· PEN
· SCISSORS

CYLINDRICAL DESKTOP PENHOLDERS
ARE A DIME A DOZEN, BUT THEY
DON'T HOLD EACH PEN AND PENCIL
SEPARATELY, AND IT WOULD BE HELPFUL
TO HOLD WIDE OBJECTS LIKE RULERS
AND FLAT OBJECTS LIKE CARDS AND
NOTEPAPER NEATLY IN PLACE TOO.
THE CROSS PEN-STAND DOES
ALL OF THESE THINGS AND
LOOKS   LIKE A
                    CROSS
REPEATING   ABOVE.
MOTIF FROM

MATERIAL:
ACRYLONITRILE-ETHYLENE-STYRENE RESIN

THIS UMBRELLA'S HANDLE MAKES IT STABLE WHEN IN USE, BUT ALSO ALLOWS IT TO STAND ON ITS OWN, HANG SECURELY FROM TABLES OR REMAIN PROPPED AGAINST A WALL WHEN NOT IN USE.

MATERIAL: NYLON
(SURFACE COATING THAT REDUCES UV RAYS BY 90%)

6.2

6.7

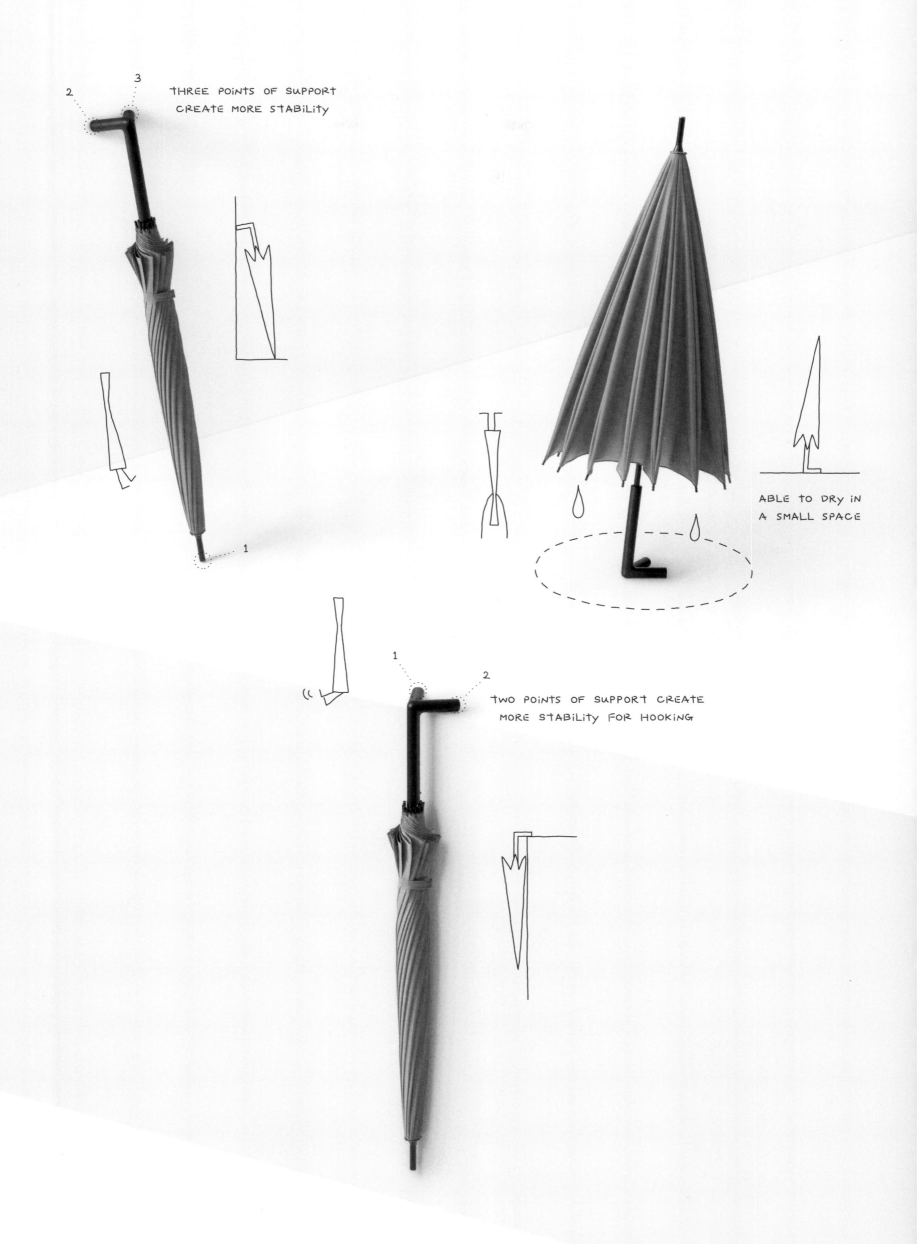

THREE POINTS OF SUPPORT
CREATE MORE STABILITY

ABLE TO DRY IN
A SMALL SPACE

TWO POINTS OF SUPPORT CREATE
MORE STABILITY FOR HOOKING

WHISTLE
RADiO

PONCHO
LANTERN

BOTTLE
CASE

AN EMERGENCY PREPAREDNESS KIT THAT INCLUDES THE BARE MiNIMUM NECESSARY FOR A CiTY-DWELLER TO MAKE iT TO A PLACE OF REFUGE DURiNG AN EARTHQUAKE OR OTHER DiSASTER. THE KiT CONTAINS A WHISTLE TO ALERT OTHERS TO ONE'S PRESENCE, A RADiO, A PONCHO, A LANTERN, A WATER BOTTLE AND A PLASTIC CASE FOR OTHER SUPPLIES, ALL PACKAGED iNSiDE A 50MM WiDE TUBE THAT iS WATERPROOF AND FLOATS.

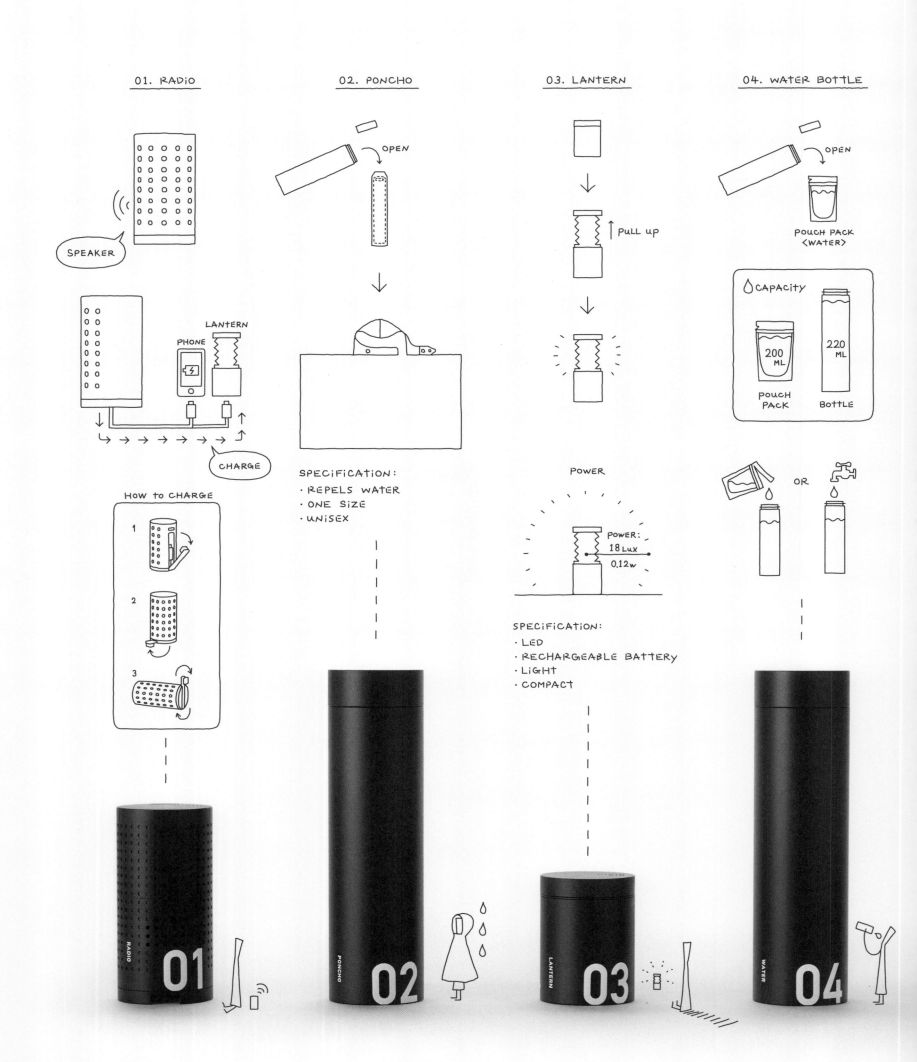

01. RADiO

SPEAKER

PHONE   LANTERN

CHARGE

How to CHARGE
1
2
3

02. PONCHO

OPEN

SPECIFICATION:
· REPELS WATER
· ONE SIZE
· UNISEX

03. LANTERN

↑ PULL UP

POWER

POWER:
18 Lux
0.12w

SPECIFICATION:
· LED
· RECHARGEABLE BATTERY
· LiGHT
· COMPACT

04. WATER BOTTLE

OPEN

POUCH PACK
⟨WATER⟩

⌾ CAPACITY

200
ML

220
ML

POUCH
PACK

BOTTLE

OR

RADiO 01   PONCHO 02   LANTERN 03   WATER 04

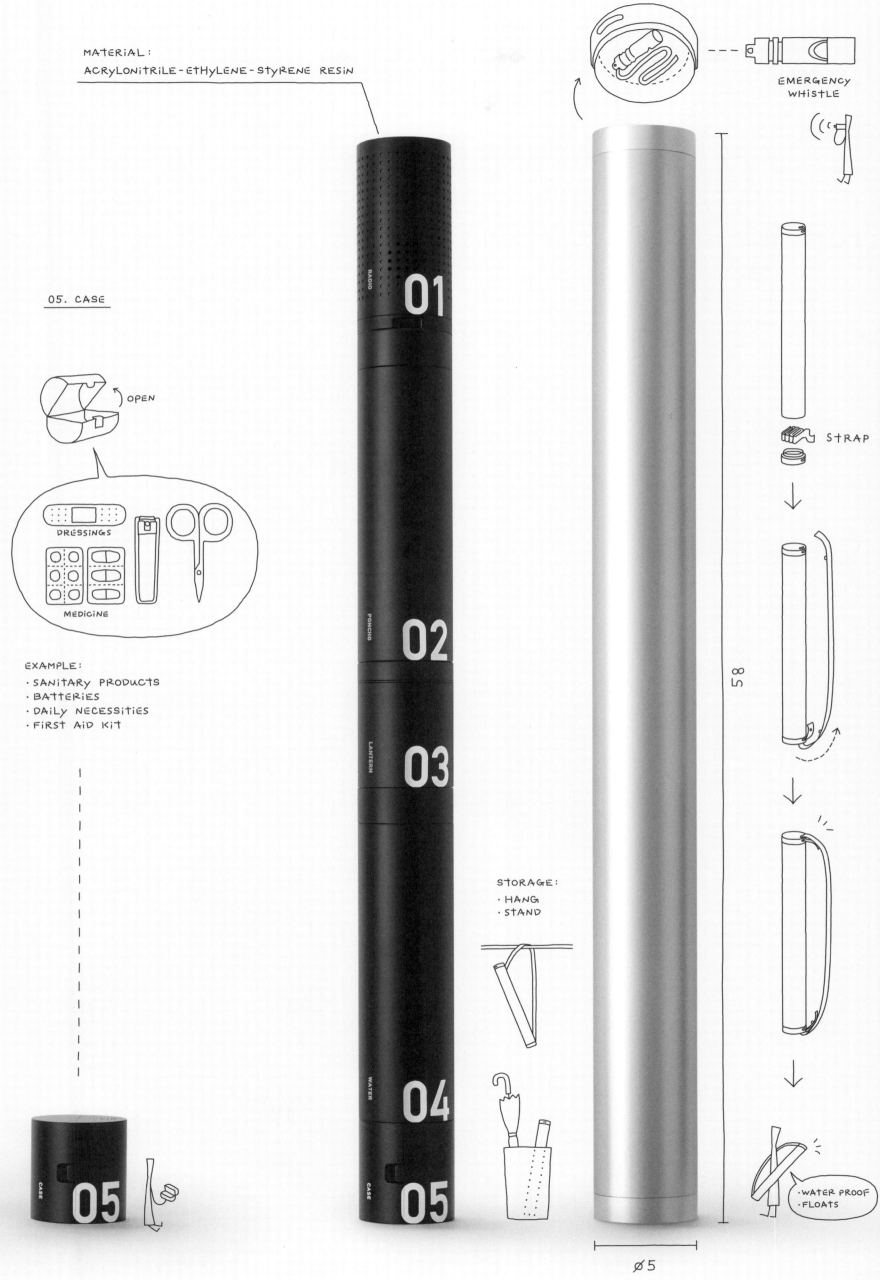

MATERIAL:
ACRYLONITRILE-ETHYLENE-STYRENE RESIN

EMERGENCY
WHISTLE

05. CASE

OPEN

DRESSINGS

MEDICINE

EXAMPLE:
· SANITARY PRODUCTS
· BATTERIES
· DAILY NECESSITIES
· FIRST AID KIT

STRAP

01
RADIO

02
PONCHO

03
LANTERN

04
WATER

05
CASE

STORAGE:
· HANG
· STAND

58

· WATER PROOF
· FLOATS

05
CASE

ø5

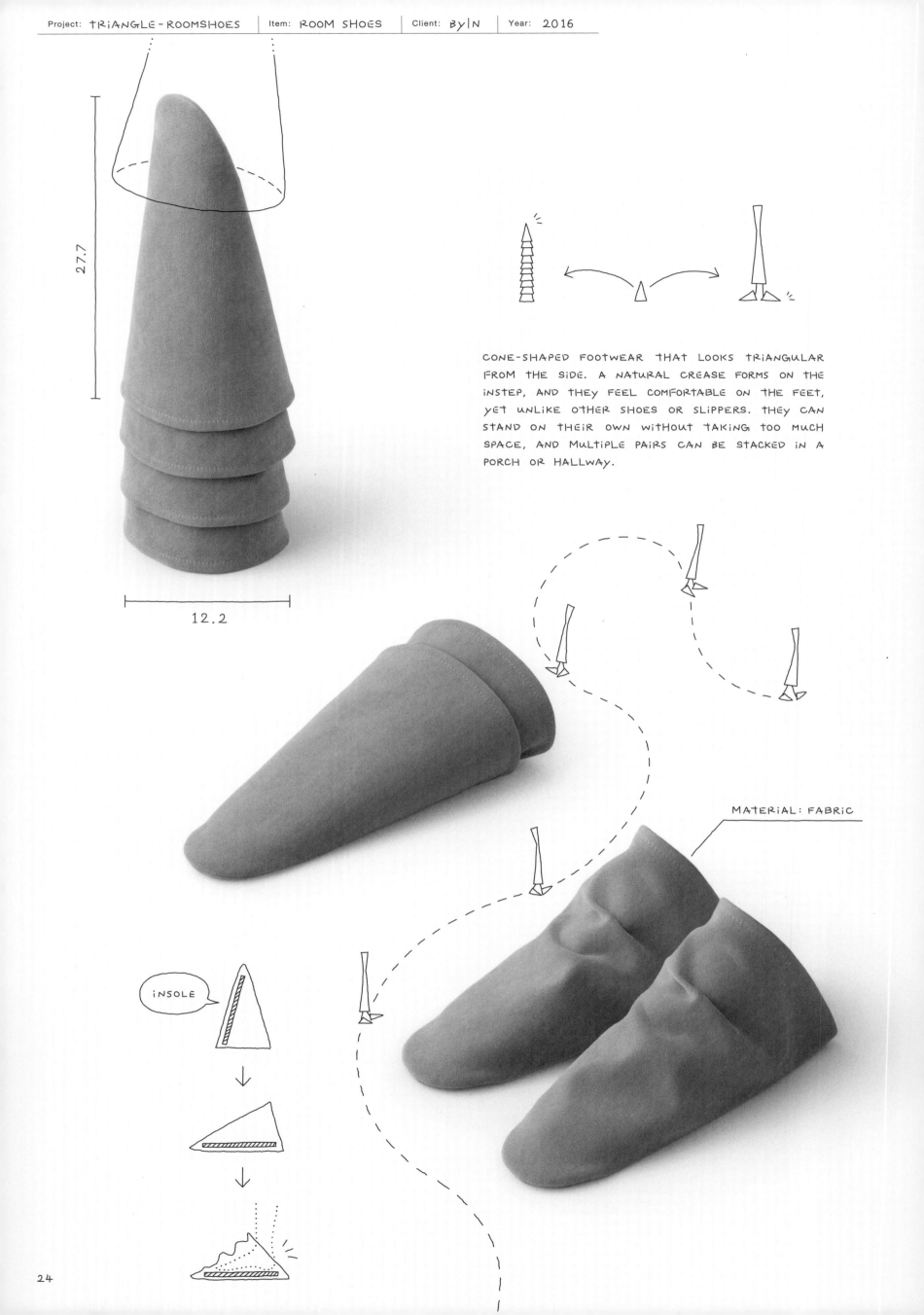

27.7

12.2

CONE-SHAPED FOOTWEAR THAT LOOKS TRIANGULAR FROM THE SIDE. A NATURAL CREASE FORMS ON THE INSTEP, AND THEY FEEL COMFORTABLE ON THE FEET, YET UNLIKE OTHER SHOES OR SLIPPERS. THEY CAN STAND ON THEIR OWN WITHOUT TAKING TOO MUCH SPACE, AND MULTIPLE PAIRS CAN BE STACKED IN A PORCH OR HALLWAY.

MATERIAL: FABRIC

INSOLE

10.5

15

5 TABS PER PAGE

STICK

FOLD

MATERIAL: PAPER

TRADITIONAL JAPANESE BOOKBINDING

EASY TO SEPARATE

THE L-SHAPED PERFORATIONS ALONG THE SIDES OF THE PAGES CAN BE FOLDED OUT TO CREATE CUSTOMIZED INDEX TABS. THE PAGES ARE FREE OF ANY LINES OR MARGINS, AND THE COVERS ARE ALL PLAIN-COLOURED AND DESIGNED TO BE AS UNOBTRUSIVE AND AESTHETICALLY PLEAS-ING AS POSSIBLE WHEN STACKED.

L-SHAPED PERFORATIONS

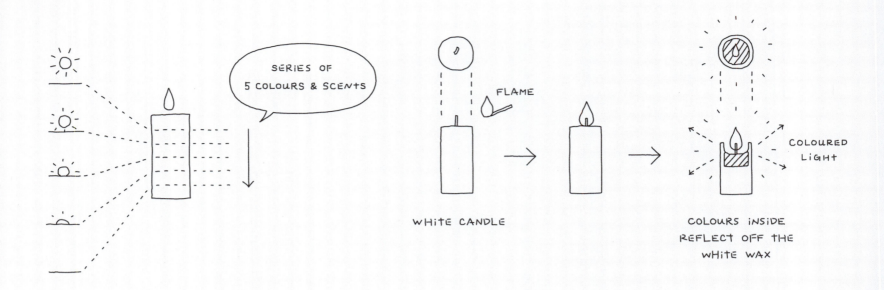

SERIES OF
5 COLOURS & SCENTS

WHITE CANDLE

FLAME

COLOURED
LIGHT

COLOURS INSIDE
REFLECT OFF THE
WHITE WAX

COLOUR – – – – WHITE – – – – – → YELLOW – – – – – – → ORANGE – – – –

SCENT – – – – / – – – – – → BERGAMOT – – – – – → LEMON GRASS – – –

TIME

10

Ø 7.5

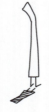

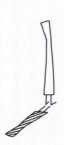

THIS LOOKS LIKE A NORMAL WHITE CANDLE. BUT ONCE LIT, THE CENTRE OF THE CANDLE BEGINS TO CHANGE COLOUR AS IT BURNS. THE TRANSITION IS INSPIRED BY THE SHIFTING SHADES OF LIGHT THAT PAINT THE SUNSET SKY. EACH COLOUR HAS A DIFFERENT SCENT. NOT ONLY DOES THE CANDLE PROVIDE LIGHT, BUT THE CHANGING COLOURS ALSO SERVE AS A REMINDER OF THE PASSAGE OF TIME.

- - - - → RED - - - - - - → PURPLE - - - - - - → BLUE - - - - - -

- - - → SWEET MARJORAM - - - - - → LAVENDER - - - - - → GERANIUM - - - -

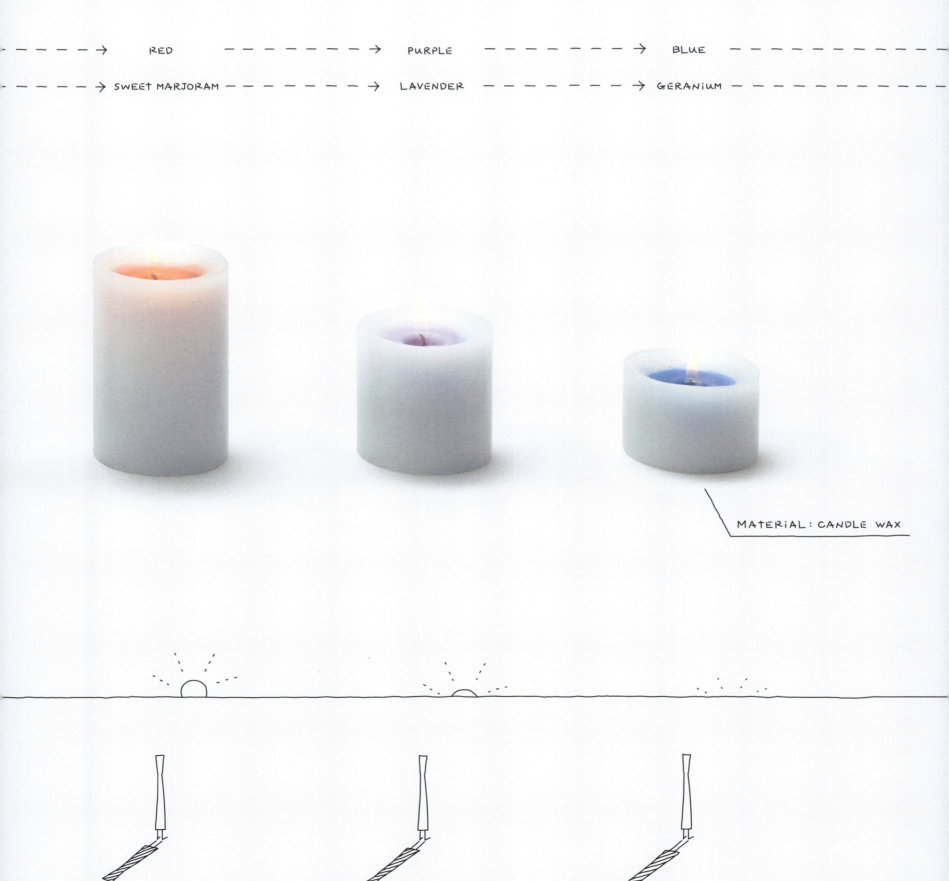

MATERIAL: CANDLE WAX

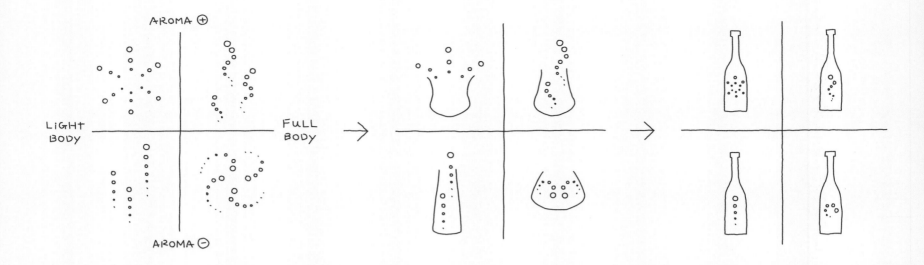

SAKE, THE JAPANESE RiCE WiNE, iS CLASSiFiED iNTO FOUR TYPES. FOUR DiFFERENT GLASSES WERE DESiGNED, EACH SPECiFICALLY TAiLORED TO A SiNGLE TYPE OF SAKE. FOUR TYPES OF SAKE WERE THEN DEVELOPED TO MATCH THE GLASS.

01.
'JyUKUSEi'
DEEP FLAVOUR

02.
'KOKU'
FULL-BODiED FLAVOUR

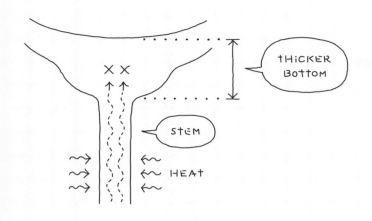

THICKER Bottom

STEM

HEAT

REDUCES THE WARMING EFFECT OF THE HANDS

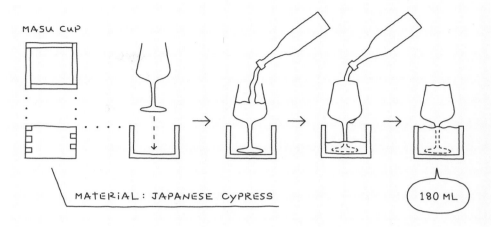

MASU CUP

MATERIAL: JAPANESE CYPRESS

180 ML

'MOKKIRI' — A TRADITIONAL STYLE OF SERVING
THE GLASS IS PLACED IN A WOODEN
MASU CUP AND THE SAKE IS POURED
UNTIL IT OVERFLOWS THE GLASS.

03.
'KAORI'
FRUITY AROMA

MATERIAL: GLASS

04.
'KEIKAI'
REFRESHING TASTE

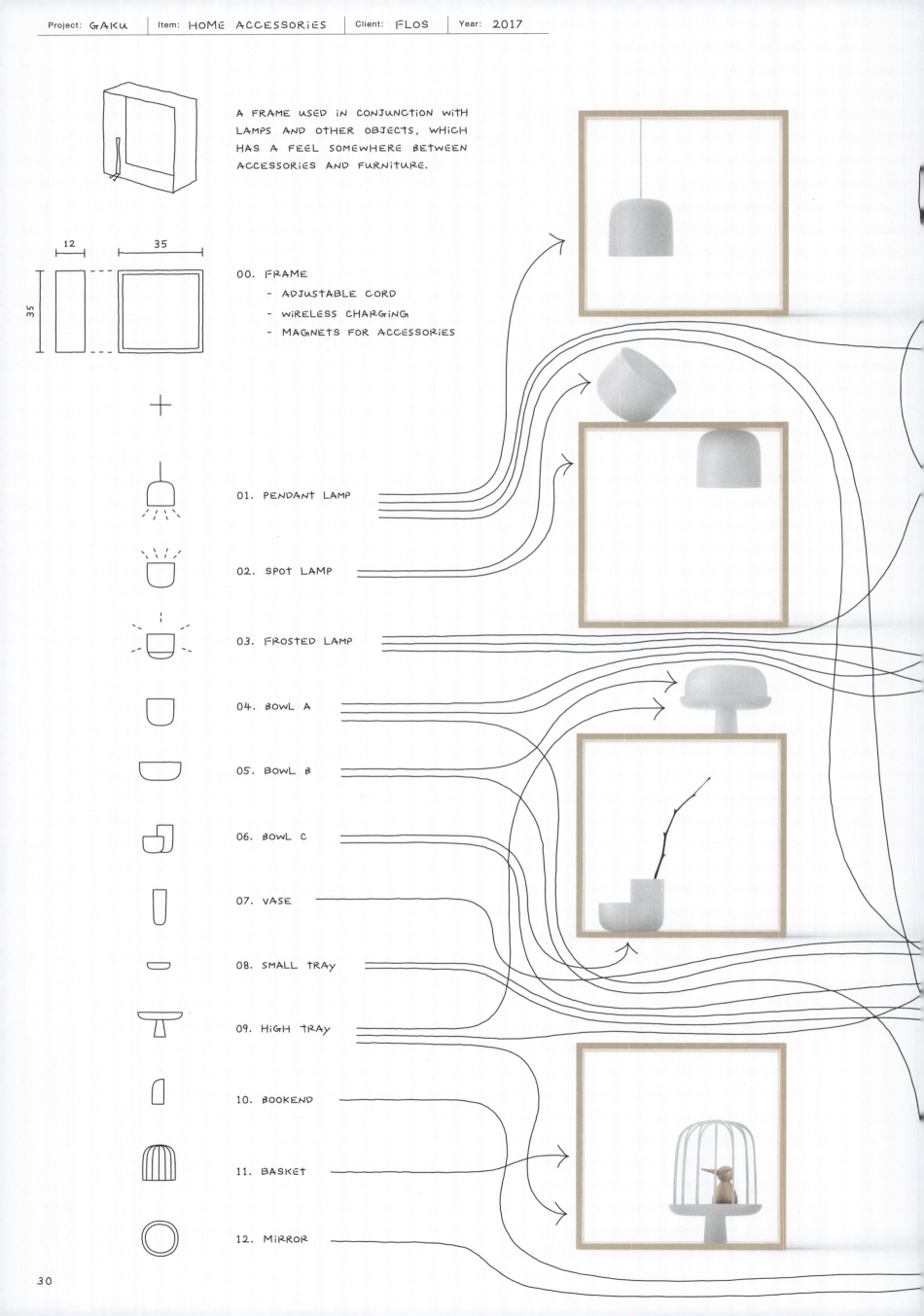

A FRAME USED IN CONJUNCTION WITH LAMPS AND OTHER OBJECTS, WHICH HAS A FEEL SOMEWHERE BETWEEN ACCESSORIES AND FURNITURE.

00. FRAME
- ADJUSTABLE CORD
- WIRELESS CHARGING
- MAGNETS FOR ACCESSORIES

01. PENDANT LAMP

02. SPOT LAMP

03. FROSTED LAMP

04. BOWL A

05. BOWL B

06. BOWL C

07. VASE

08. SMALL TRAY

09. HIGH TRAY

10. BOOKEND

11. BASKET

12. MIRROR

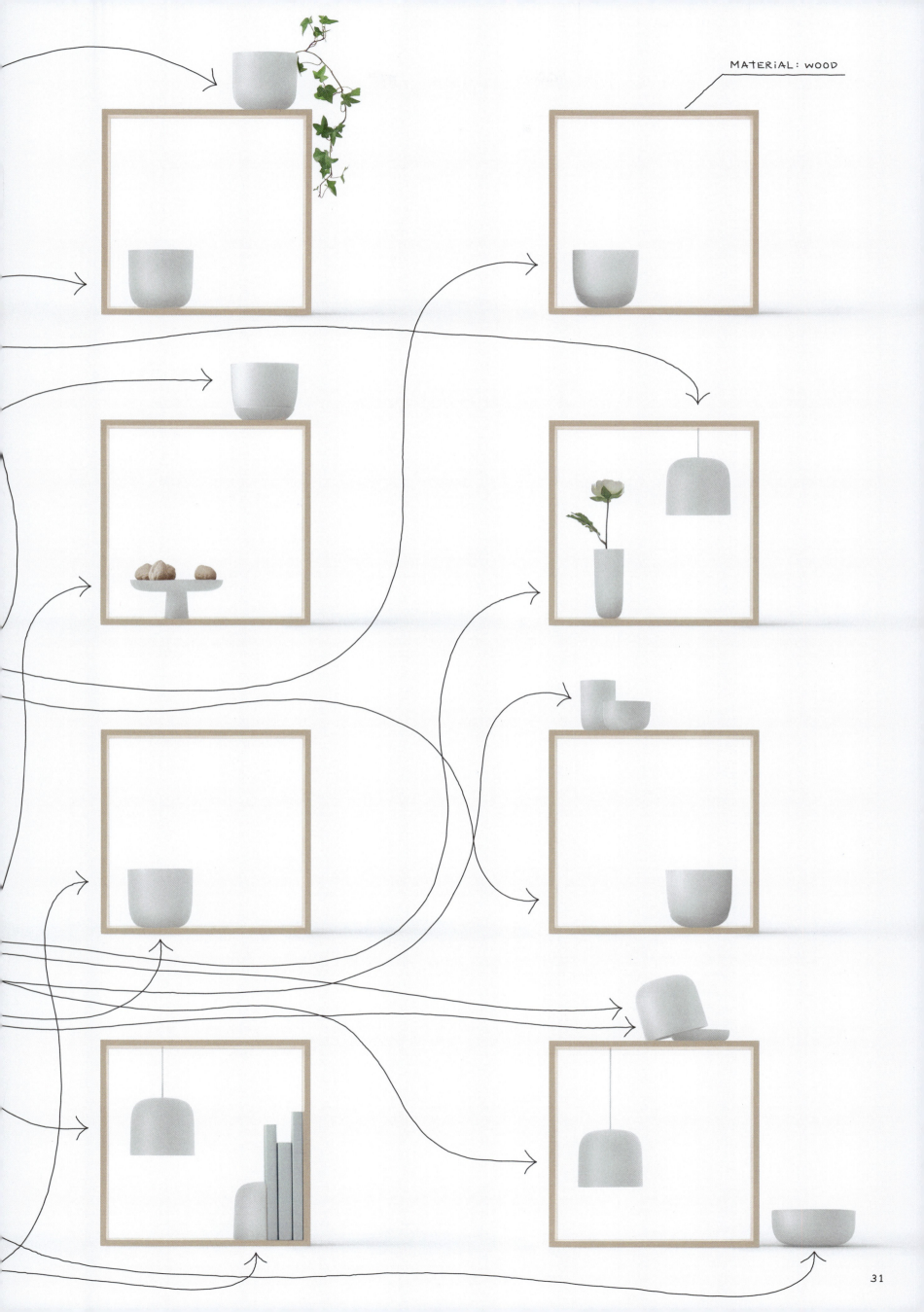

MATERIAL: WOOD

01. CROSSED ZiPPERS

UNLiKE ORDiNARY ZiPPERS, WHiCH CAN ONLY BE OPENED OR CLOSED iN ONE DiRECTiON, ONE ZiPPER CAN BE CROSSED WiTH ANOTHER ONE AT A RiGHT ANGLE, ENABLiNG THEM TO BE OPENED AND CLOSED LENGTHWiSE AND WiDTHWiSE. THE iNTERSECTiON POiNT OF THE ZiPPERS iS FiXED BY USiNG FOUR SMALL SNAP-ON ELEMENTS.

MATERiAL: NYLON

iDEA FOR A BAG?

02. ZiPPER WiTH GAPS

WHiLE RETAiNiNG THE TYPiCAL USABiLiTY OF A ZiPPER, NEW FUNCTiONS ARE MADE POSSiBLE BY FASTENiNG AT 'POiNTS', RATHER THAN iN A LiNE. THE GAPS CREATE BREATHABiLiTY, FLEXiBiLiTY, AND A WAY TO PASS CORDS OR CABLES THROUGH. ELEMENTS FASTEN ON TOP OF EACH OTHER LiKE STUDS OR BUTTONS, RATHER THAN SiDE BY SiDE.

OPEN

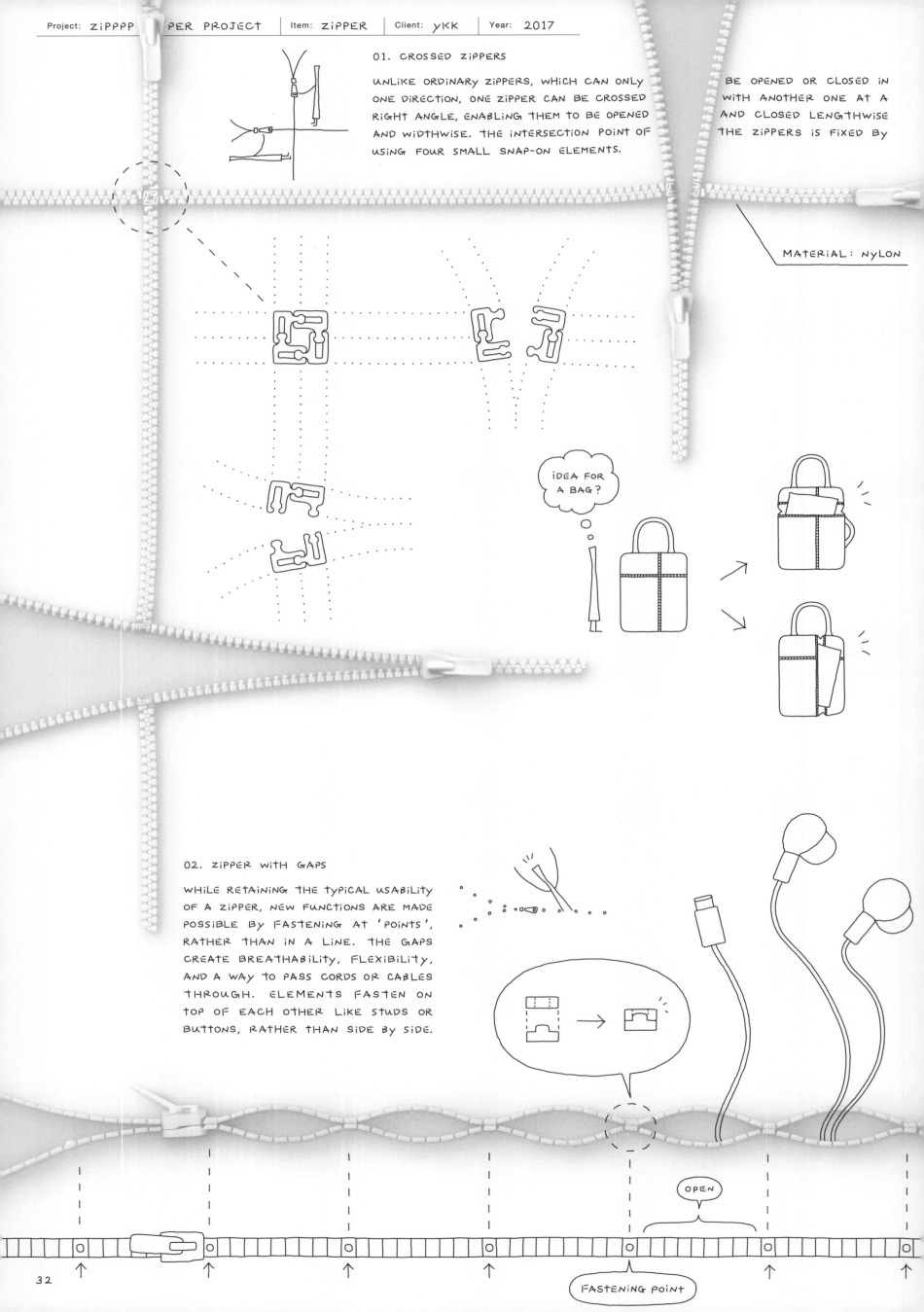

FASTENiNG POiNT

03. ZIPPER WITH A ROTATING MOTION

WITH A STANDARD ZIPPER, THE SLIDER IS PULLED WITH ONE HAND, WHILE THE OTHER HAND HOLDS THE BOTTOM OF THE FABRIC TO KEEP THE ZIPPER STRAIGHT, ALLOWING IT TO OPEN AND CLOSE SMOOTHLY. THIS MAY BE DIFFICULT FOR SOME USERS, SO THE PROBLEM HAS BEEN RESOLVED BY REPLACING THE LINEAR, MOTION WITH A ROTATING MOTION. WHEN THE DISC-LIKE SLIDER IS TURNED, INTERNAL GEARS CLAMP THE ELEMENTS AND THEY OPEN OR CLOSE SIMULTANEOUSLY.

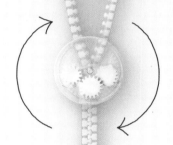

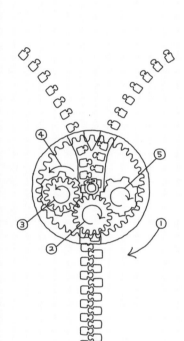

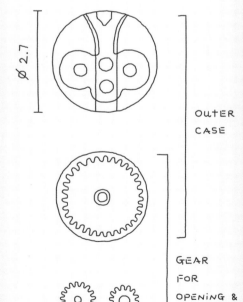

Ø 2.7

OUTER CASE

GEAR FOR OPENING & CLOSING

GEAR FOR MOVING UP & DOWN

THE GEARS ALLOW ONE-HANDED OPENING OR CLOSING, WITH LESS EFFORT

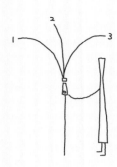

04. ZIPPER TO CONNECT THREE ELEMENTS

BY MOVING A THREE-PRONGED SLIDER, THREE SETS OF ZIPPER ELEMENTS ARE MESHED TOGETHER, MAKING IT POSSIBLE TO GO BEYOND TWO DIMENSIONS AND CONNECT FABRICS THREE DIMENSIONALLY. THREE EDGES CAN BE SIMULTANEOUSLY SEPARATED OR JOINED AT THE SAME POINT.

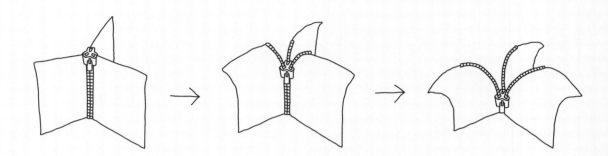

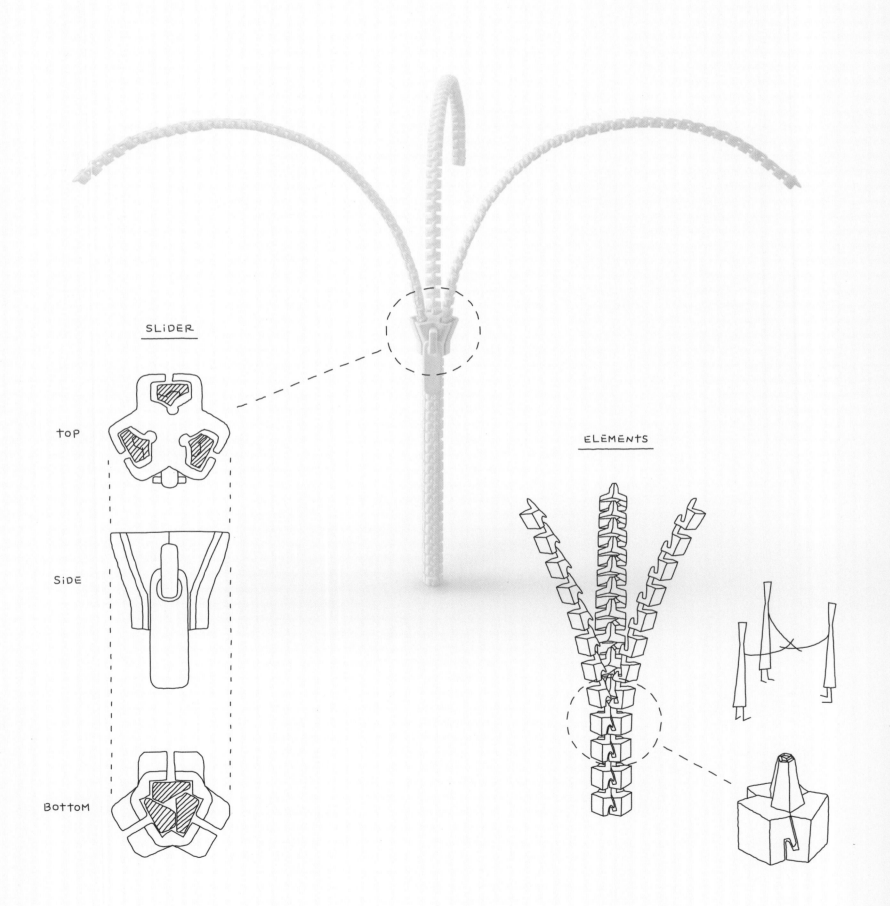

SLIDER

TOP

SIDE

BOTTOM

ELEMENTS

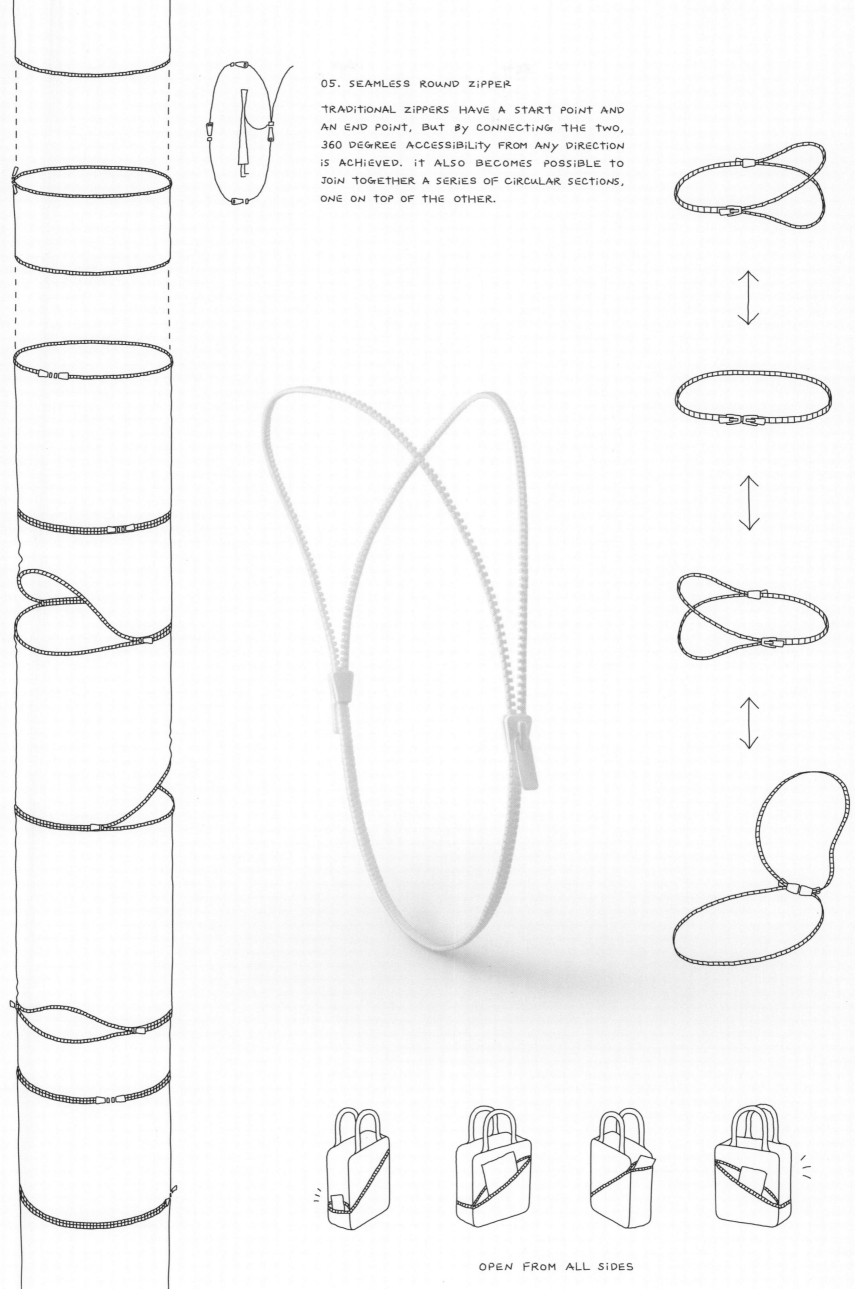

05. SEAMLESS ROUND ZIPPER

TRADITIONAL ZIPPERS HAVE A START POINT AND AN END POINT, BUT BY CONNECTING THE TWO, 360 DEGREE ACCESSIBILITY FROM ANY DIRECTION IS ACHIEVED. IT ALSO BECOMES POSSIBLE TO JOIN TOGETHER A SERIES OF CIRCULAR SECTIONS, ONE ON TOP OF THE OTHER.

OPEN FROM ALL SIDES

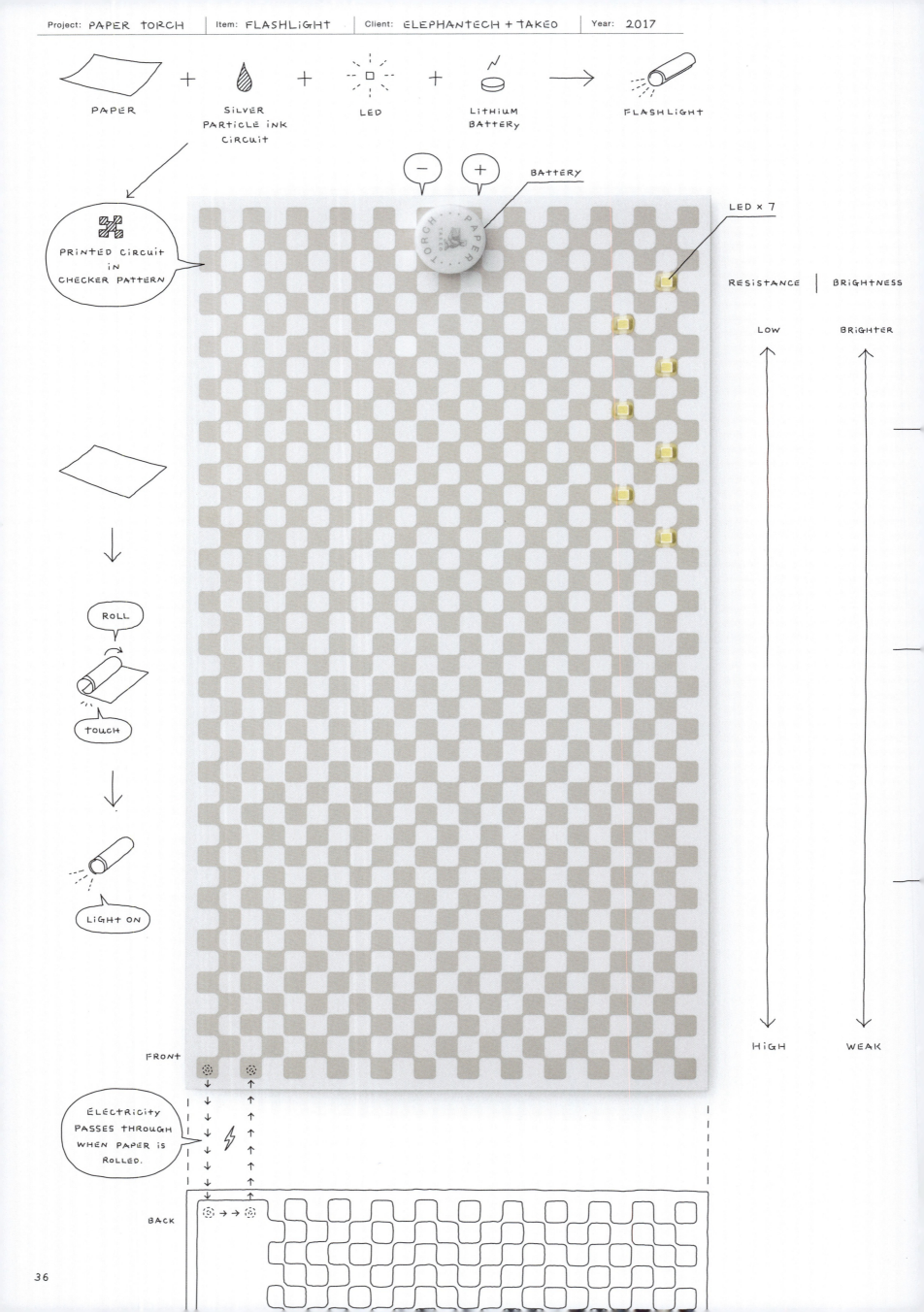

PAPER + SILVER PARTICLE INK CIRCUIT + LED + LITHIUM BATTERY → FLASHLIGHT

PRINTED CIRCUIT IN CHECKER PATTERN

BATTERY

− +

LED × 7

RESISTANCE | BRIGHTNESS

LOW | BRIGHTER

HIGH | WEAK

ROLL

TOUCH

LIGHT ON

FRONT

ELECTRICITY PASSES THROUGH WHEN PAPER IS ROLLED.

BACK

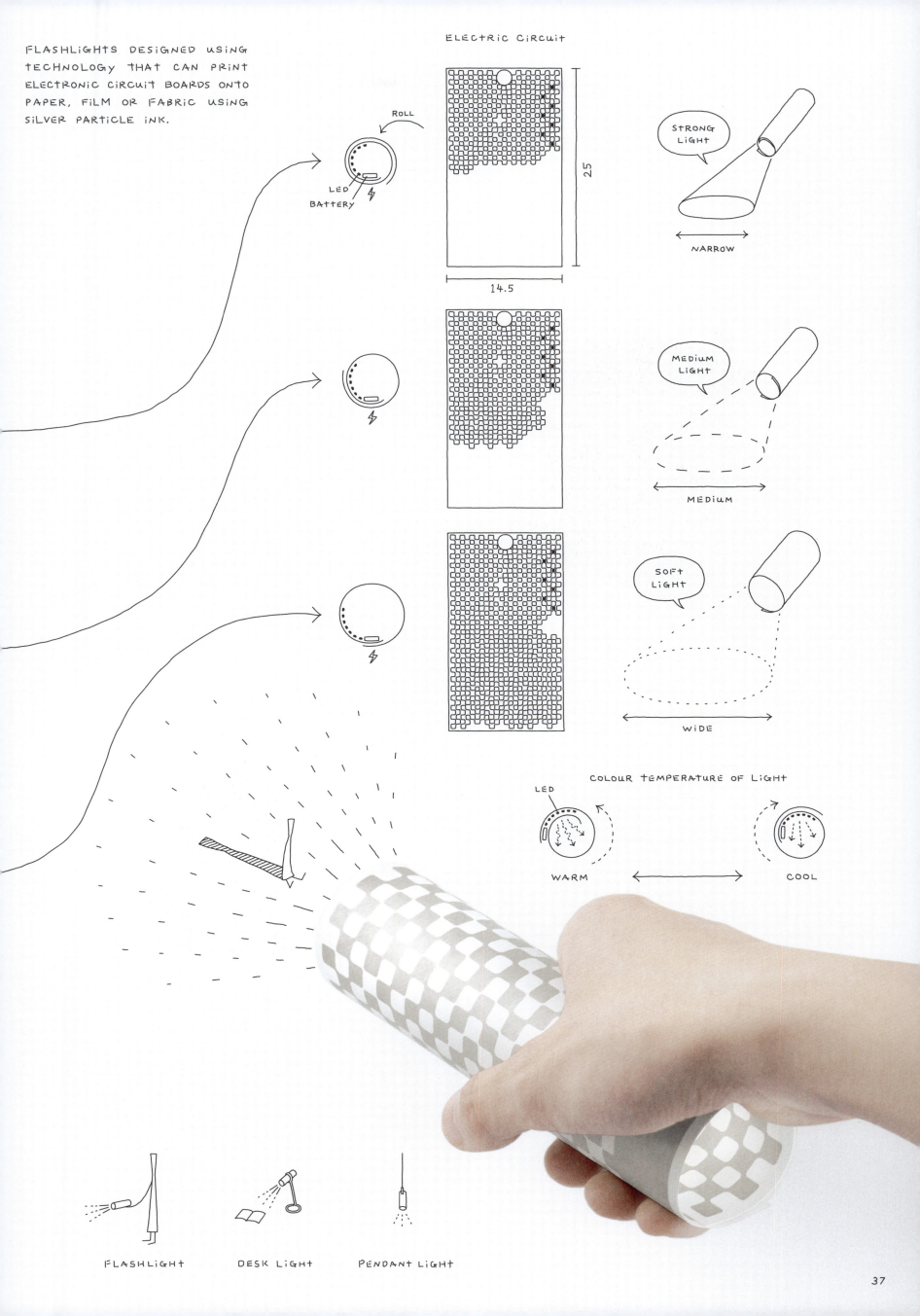

FLASHLIGHTS DESIGNED USING
TECHNOLOGY THAT CAN PRINT
ELECTRONIC CIRCUIT BOARDS ONTO
PAPER, FILM OR FABRIC USING
SILVER PARTICLE INK.

ELECTRIC CIRCUIT

ROLL

LED
BATTERY

25

14.5

STRONG
LIGHT

NARROW

MEDIUM
LIGHT

MEDIUM

SOFT
LIGHT

WIDE

COLOUR TEMPERATURE OF LIGHT

LED

WARM

COOL

FLASHLIGHT   DESK LIGHT   PENDANT LIGHT

37

thick & uneven

thin & even

PORCELAIN CRAFTED BY HIGHLY-SKILLED ARTISANS HAS VERY LITTLE DISTORTION AND IT IS SAID THAT THE THINNEST, MOST UNIFORM PIECES PRODUCE THE CLEAREST, MOST BEAUTIFUL RINGING SOUND. BECAUSE OF THIS, THE ARTISANS CHECK THE QUALITY OF THEIR PIECES BY LIGHTLY FLICKING THE PORCELAIN'S SURFACE.

7.9

Ø 3.5

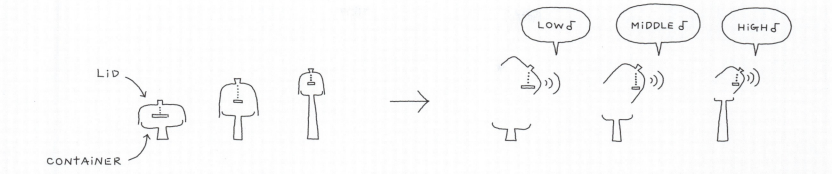

THESE CONTAINERS INCORPORATE A LID THAT RINGS LIKE A BELL. A DELICATE CRYSTAL-CLEAR RINGING CAN BE HEARD EACH TIME THE LID IS REMOVED TO ACCESS THE ACCESSORIES OR SNACKS STORED INSIDE. THE SMALL CONTAINERS ARE AVAILABLE IN FIVE DIFFERENT SIZE AND HEIGHT COMBINATIONS THAT EACH PRODUCES ITS OWN UNIQUE TONE, ALLOWING USERS TO EXPERIENCE BEAUTY IN SIGHT AND SOUND FORM.

MATERIAL: CERAMIC

'KONA-SHOYU' IS A NEW TYPE OF POWDERED (= KONA)
SOY SAUCE (= SHOYU) SEASONING. UNLIKE LIQUID SOY SAUCE,
IT DOES NOT MAKE FOOD DAMP, AND CONSEQUENTLY HELPS
DEEP-FRIED DISHES TO MAINTAIN THEIR CRISPNESS.

SOY SAUCE

POWDERED SOY SAUCE

MATERIAL:
ACRYLONITRILE-ETHYLENE-
STYRENE RESIN

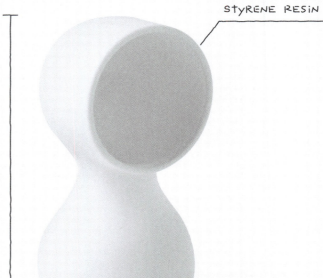

8.5

4

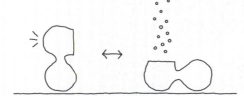

THE BACK OF THE CONTAINER
IS SLIGHTLY FLATTENED SO IT
CAN BE EASILY LAID DOWN
WHEN REFILLING.

CAP

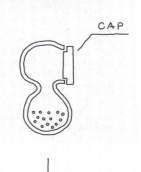

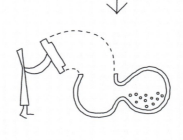

CHECK
AMOUNT

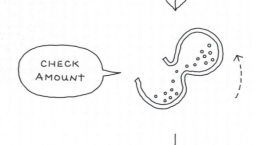

SERVE

40

THIS CUTLERY SET HAS BEEN REDUCED TO THE ABSOLUTE MINIMUM, LIMITING THE AMOUNT OF MATERIAL USED WHILE STILL RETAINING FUNCTIONALITY. ALL THAT REMAINS IS THE OUTLINE OF THE CUTLERY, LIKE THE IMAGE OF A SKELETON IN AN X-RAY. THERE ARE FOUR ITEMS: SPOON, FORK, KNIFE, AND TEASPOON.

MATERIAL: STAINLESS STEEL
FINISH: PVD COATED

22

HANG   HOOK   LAY   LEAN

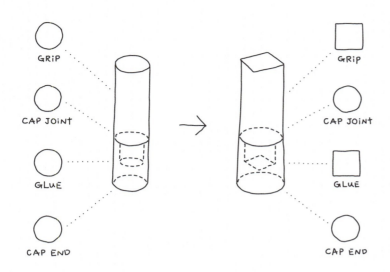

GRIP

CAP JOINT

GLUE

CAP END

GRIP

CAP JOINT

GLUE

CAP END

GLUE STICKS USUALLY HAVE A CYLINDRICAL SHAPE, BUT ARE DIFFICULT TO APPLY TO THE CORNERS OF PAPER. THE STICK WAS THEREFORE CHANGED TO A SQUARE SHAPE AND THE CASE WAS DESIGNED USING A COMBINATION OF SQUARE AND ROUND SHAPES TO IMPROVE FUNCTIONALITY AND COMFORT OF USE.

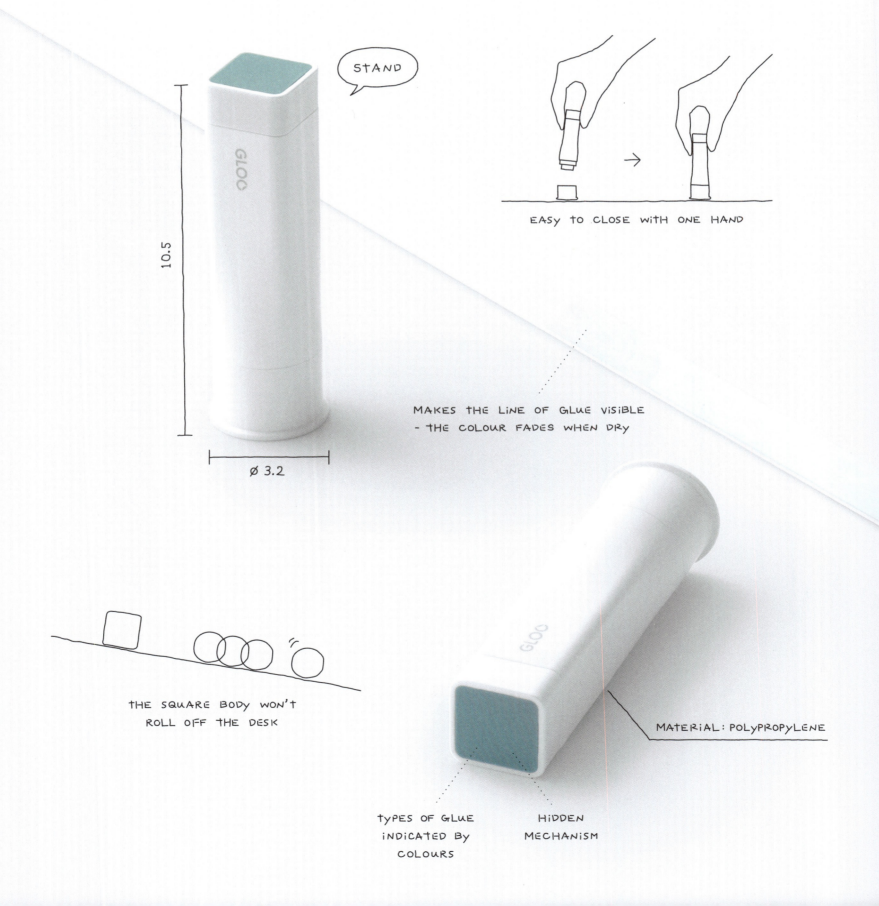

STAND

10.5

Ø 3.2

EASY TO CLOSE WITH ONE HAND

MAKES THE LINE OF GLUE VISIBLE
- THE COLOUR FADES WHEN DRY

THE SQUARE BODY WON'T
ROLL OFF THE DESK

MATERIAL: POLYPROPYLENE

TYPES OF GLUE
INDICATED BY
COLOURS

HIDDEN
MECHANISM

THE KNOB TO SQUEEZE
OUT THE GLUE IS
EASIER TO GRASP

AS A SQUARE CAP WAS
FOUND TO HAVE LOW SEAL-
ABILITY, A UNIQUE ROUND
CAP WAS DEVELOPED TO
OVERCOME THIS ISSUE.

TO PREVENT SPILLED
ADHESIVE FROM HARDENING,
A CAVITY IS PROVIDED INSIDE

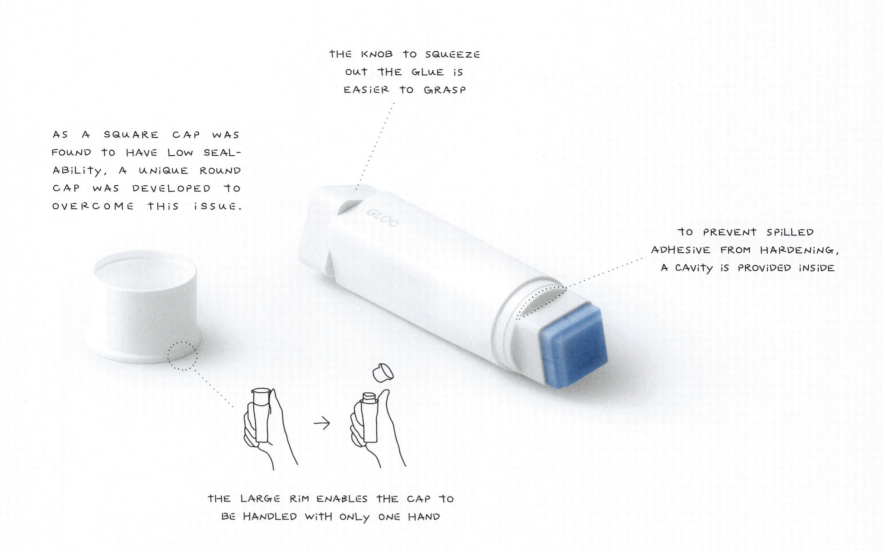

THE LARGE RIM ENABLES THE CAP TO
BE HANDLED WITH ONLY ONE HAND

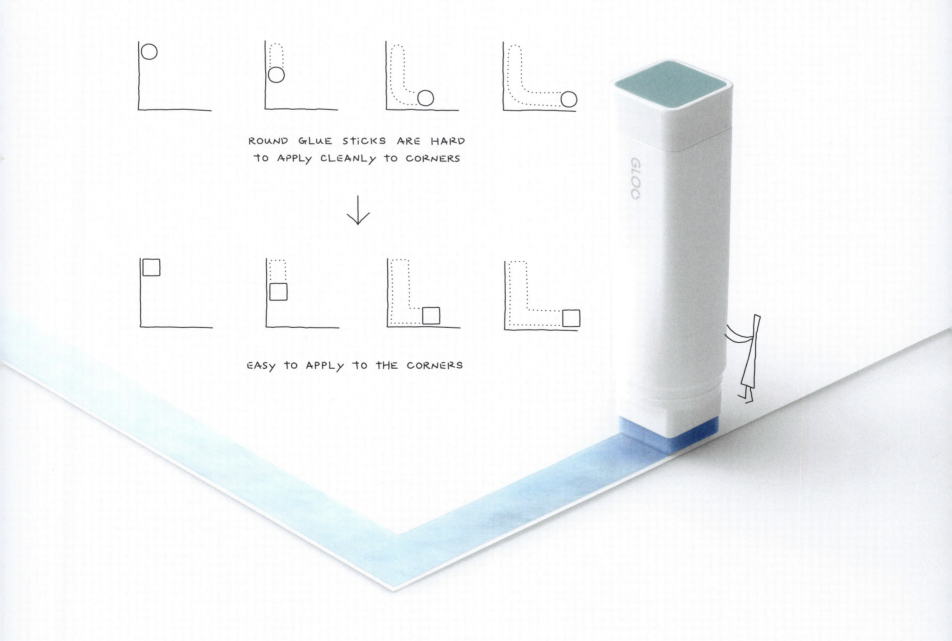

ROUND GLUE STICKS ARE HARD
TO APPLY CLEANLY TO CORNERS

EASY TO APPLY TO THE CORNERS

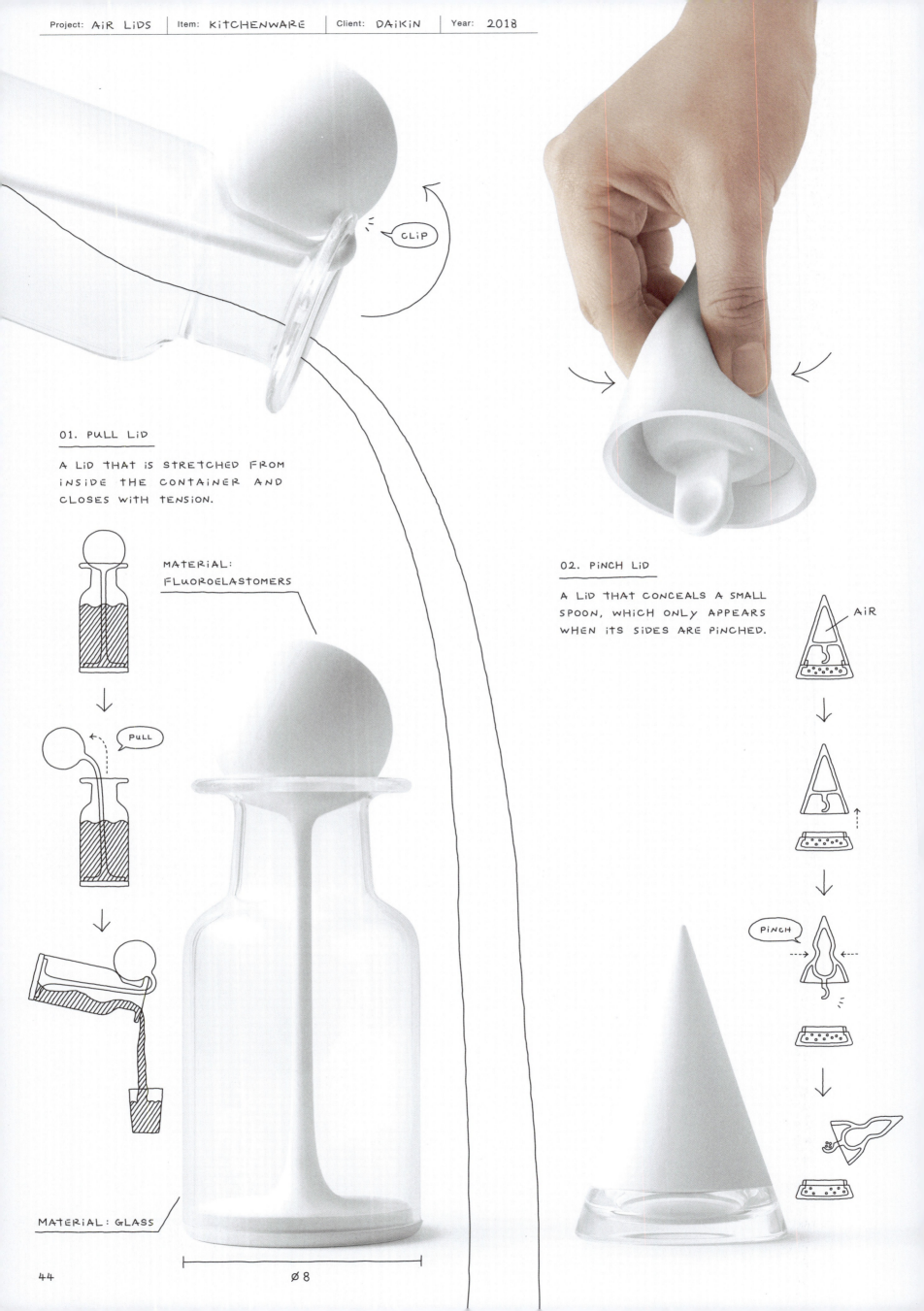

CLIP

01. PULL LiD

A LiD THAT iS STRETCHED FROM INSIDE THE CONTAINER AND CLOSES WITH TENSION.

MATERIAL: FLUOROELASTOMERS

PULL

MATERIAL: GLASS

02. PiNCH LiD

A LiD THAT CONCEALS A SMALL SPOON, WHiCH ONLY APPEARS WHEN iTS SiDES ARE PiNCHED.

AiR

PiNCH

Ø 8

A KITCHENWARE COLLECTION
ELASTOMERS. FLUOROELA-
WITH OUTSTANDING
THEIR COLOUR

FOCUSED ON DIFFERENT LID DESIGNS USING FLUORO-
STOMERS ARE A TYPE OF HIGH-PERFORMANCE RUBBER
HEAT, OIL AND ACID RESISTANCE, WHICH RETAIN
AND SHAPE OVER A LONG PERIOD OF TIME.

04. PUSH LID

A LID THAT IS PUSHED DOWN
TO RELEASE LIQUID FROM
THE CONTAINER.

03. PRESS LID

A LID FOR LIQUID
CONTAINERS THAT
OPENS LIKE A MOUTH
WHEN ITS TOP IS
PRESSED DOWN.

05. PICK-UP LID

A LID THAT CAN PICK UP A PINCH
OF SEASONING FROM A CONTAINER.

FLUOROPOLYMERS ARE MOLECULES PRODUCED BY [...] COMPRESSING AND HEATING GRANULATED FLUORITE, WHICH IS A [...] NATURAL MINERAL. THEY HAVE HIGH WEAR-RESISTANCE AND [...] ANTIFOULING PRO-PERTIES, SO THEIR APPEARANCE REMAINS [...] UNDAMAGED FOR EXTENDED PERIODS. THIS MATERIAL IS [...] COMMONLY USED IN THE MEDICAL INDUSTRY AND IN JOINTS FOR [...] ROBOTS, BECAUSE OF ITS EXTREMELY LOW FRICTION. ALTHOUGH VERY HIGH- [...] TECH, ITS WEIGHT AND WARMTH HAVE A NATURAL AND TACTILE FEEL. [...] THE SEARCH OF A NEW APPLICATION FOR THIS MATERIAL [...] AND ITS SPECIAL QUALI-TIES LED TO THE DESIGN OF THIS COLLECTION. WHEN [...] CLOSED, THESE ALL-WHITE CASES HAVE THE SAME SPHERICAL SHAPE, 65MM IN [...] DIAMETER, BUT EACH CASE HAS SLIGHT INDENTATIONS IN A DIFFERENT PLACE. [...] THESE INDENTATIONS SERVE AS A CLUE AS TO HOW THE BOXES OPEN. EACH [...] CASE SLIDES OPEN IN A UNIQUE WAY, REVEALING THE JEWELRY WITHIN.

Ø 6.5

MATERIAL: FLUOROPOLYMER

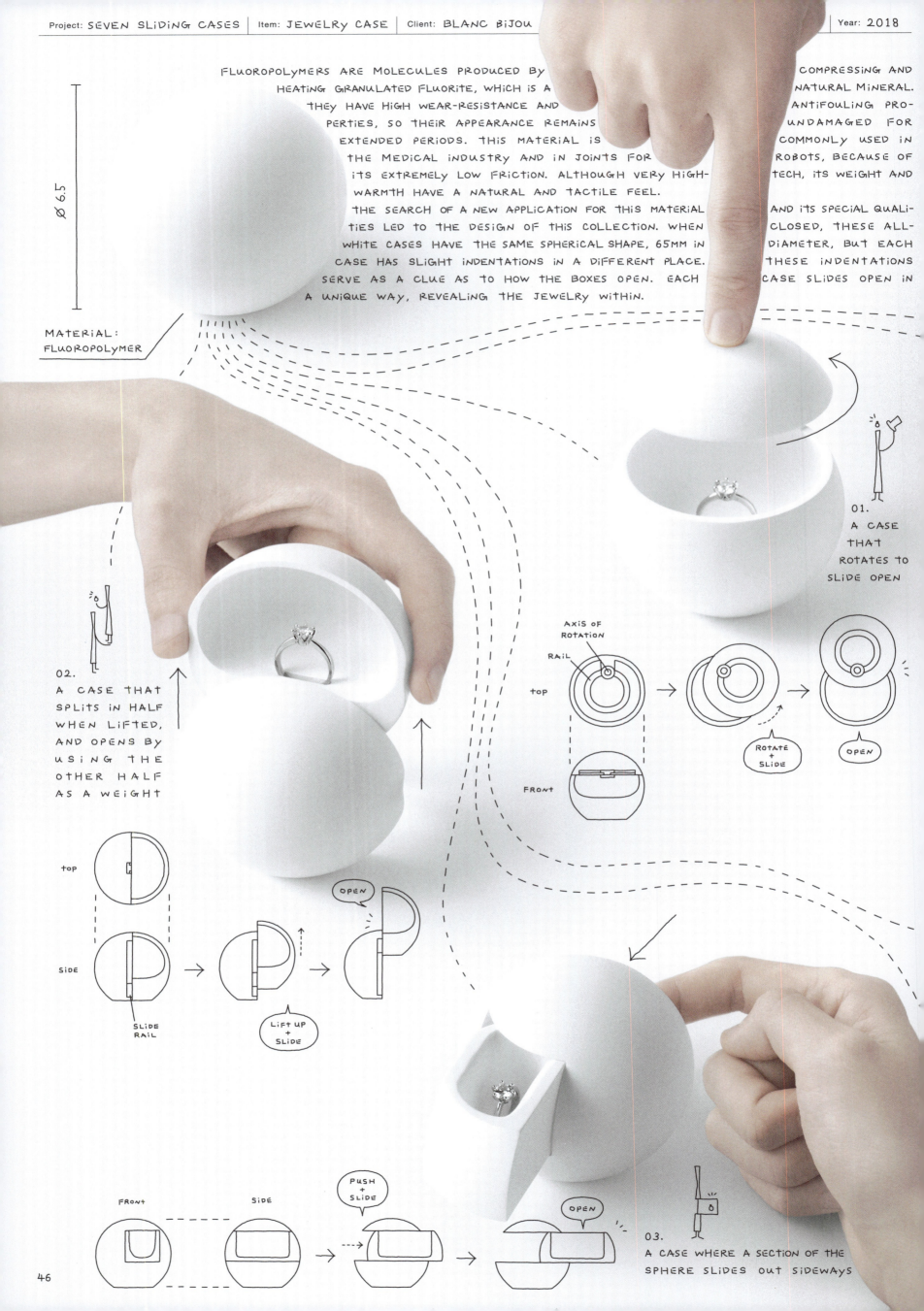

01. A CASE THAT ROTATES TO SLIDE OPEN

AXIS OF ROTATION
RAIL
top
FRONT
ROTATE + SLIDE
OPEN

02. A CASE THAT SPLITS IN HALF WHEN LIFTED, AND OPENS BY USING THE OTHER HALF AS A WEIGHT

top
SIDE
SLIDE RAIL
LIFT UP + SLIDE
OPEN

FRONT
SIDE
PUSH + SLIDE
OPEN

03. A CASE WHERE A SECTION OF THE SPHERE SLIDES OUT SIDEWAYS

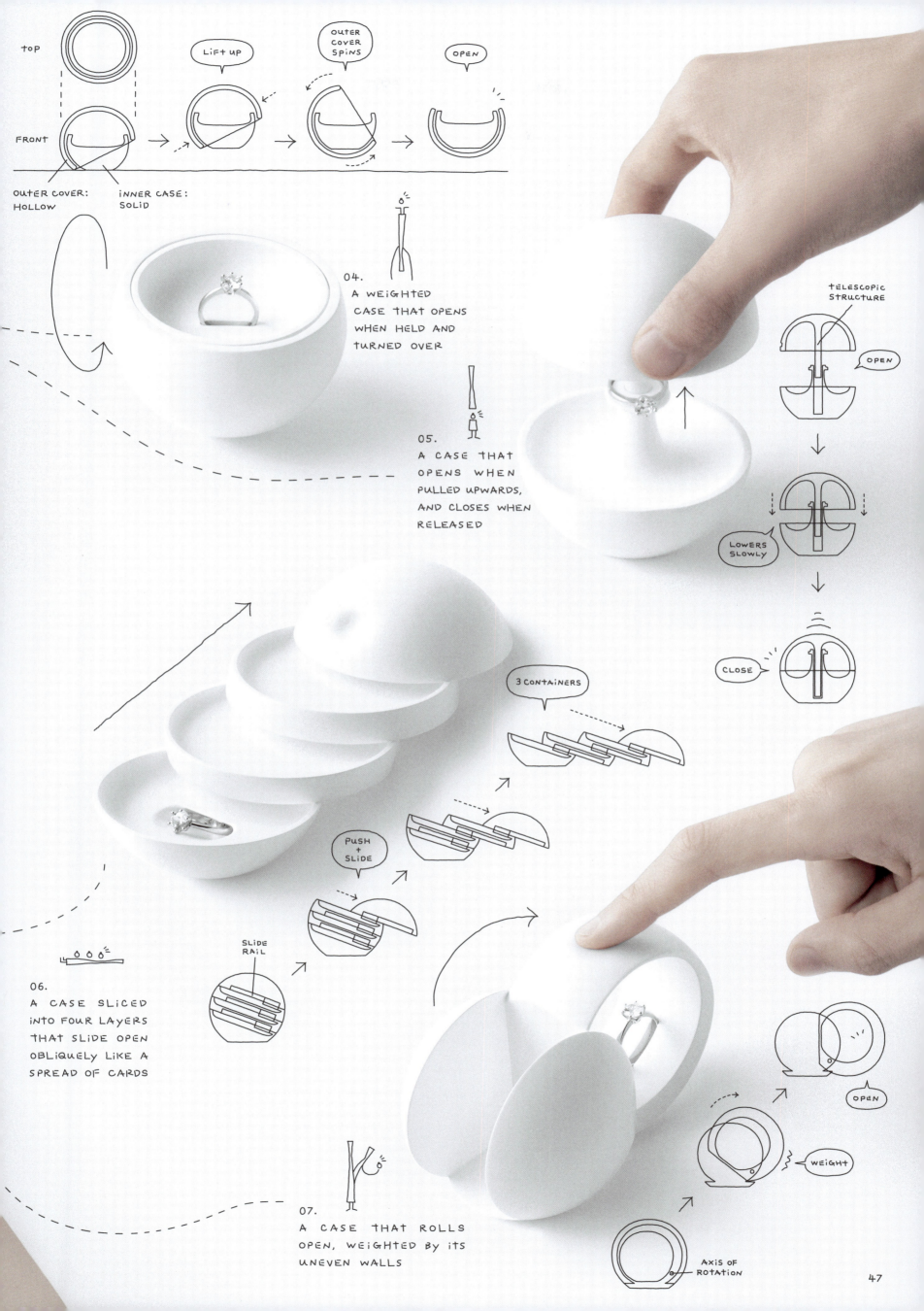

FiNER GRiNDiNG

AROMATiC QUALiTiES

PEPPER MiLL < PESTLE & MORTAR

PESTLE + MORTAR + CONTAiNER

8.5

3.1

6

MATERiAL: GLASS
FiNiSH: FROSTED

CROSS SECTiON

EASY TO GRiP

THiCKER BOTTOM
iNCREASES STRENGTH

LiD

PEPPER

GRiND

DRiED PEPPERCORNS ARE POURED OUT
OF THE CONTAiNER ONTO THE BASE.
THE BOTTOM OF THE CONTAiNER iS
THEN USED AS A 'PESTLE' AND iTS
BASE iS USED AS THE 'MORTAR' TO
GRiND THE PEPPER.

RiDGES

COARSE ⟷ FiNE

RANGE OF GRiNDiNG

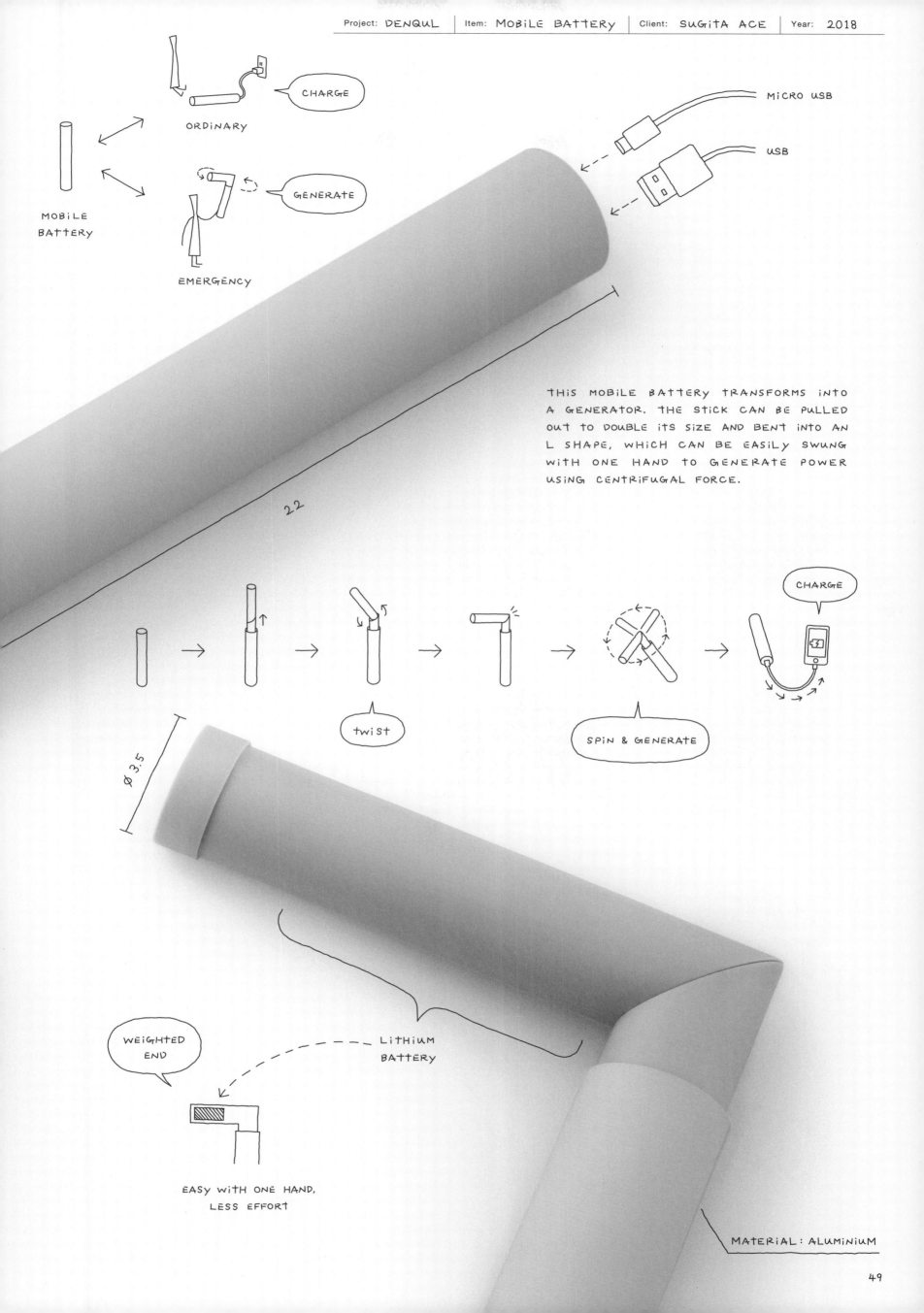

CHARGE

ORDINARY

GENERATE

MOBILE BATTERY

EMERGENCY

MICRO USB

USB

THIS MOBILE BATTERY TRANSFORMS INTO A GENERATOR. THE STICK CAN BE PULLED OUT TO DOUBLE ITS SIZE AND BENT INTO AN L SHAPE, WHICH CAN BE EASILY SWUNG WITH ONE HAND TO GENERATE POWER USING CENTRIFUGAL FORCE.

22

Ø 3.5

TWIST

SPIN & GENERATE

CHARGE

WEIGHTED END

LITHIUM BATTERY

EASY WITH ONE HAND, LESS EFFORT

MATERIAL: ALUMINIUM

A COMMEMORATIVE GIFT FOR THE 2019 RUGBY WORLD CUP IN JAPAN, GIVEN OUT TO BUSINESS LEADERS AND VIPS FROM AROUND THE WORLD WHO CAME TO JAPAN TO WATCH THE TOURNAMENT.

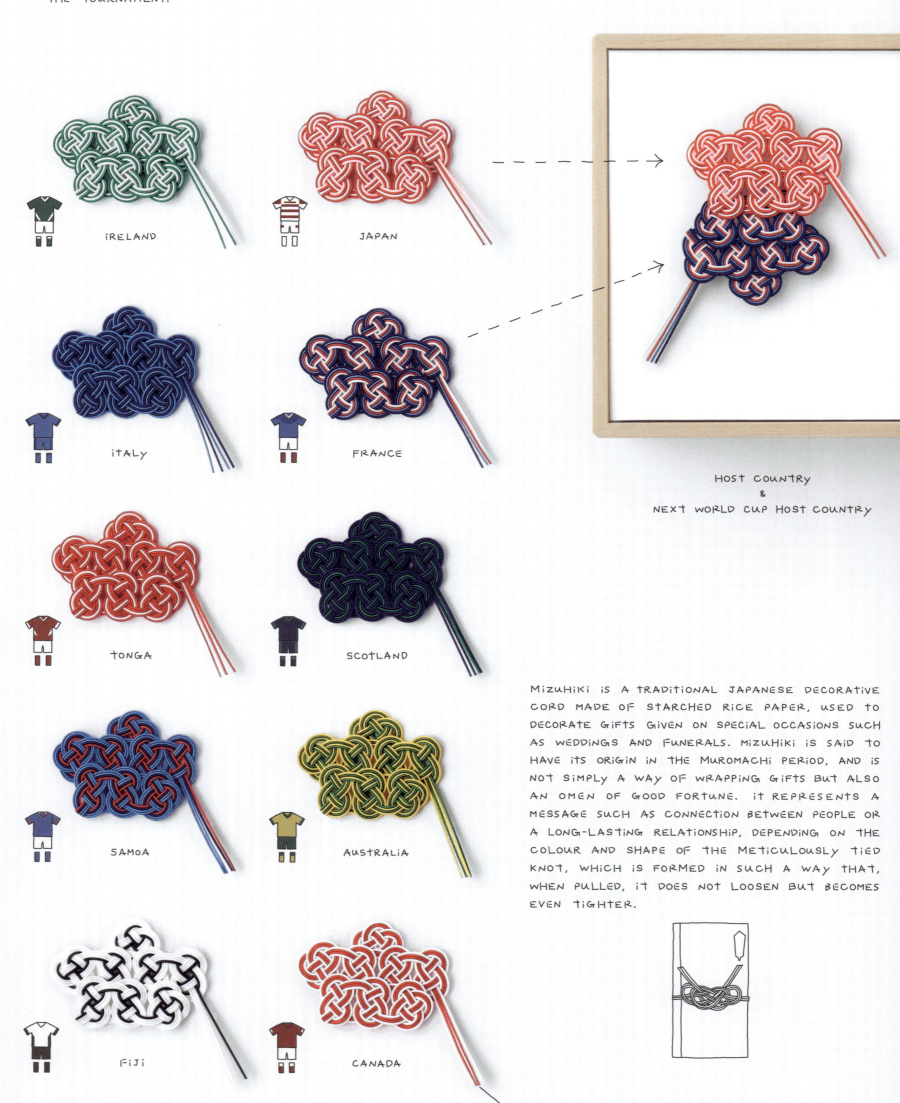

IRELAND

JAPAN

ITALY

FRANCE

HOST COUNTRY
&
NEXT WORLD CUP HOST COUNTRY

TONGA

SCOTLAND

SAMOA

AUSTRALIA

MIZUHIKI IS A TRADITIONAL JAPANESE DECORATIVE CORD MADE OF STARCHED RICE PAPER, USED TO DECORATE GIFTS GIVEN ON SPECIAL OCCASIONS SUCH AS WEDDINGS AND FUNERALS. MIZUHIKI IS SAID TO HAVE ITS ORIGIN IN THE MUROMACHI PERIOD, AND IS NOT SIMPLY A WAY OF WRAPPING GIFTS BUT ALSO AN OMEN OF GOOD FORTUNE. IT REPRESENTS A MESSAGE SUCH AS CONNECTION BETWEEN PEOPLE OR A LONG-LASTING RELATIONSHIP, DEPENDING ON THE COLOUR AND SHAPE OF THE METICULOUSLY TIED KNOT, WHICH IS FORMED IN SUCH A WAY THAT, WHEN PULLED, IT DOES NOT LOOSEN BUT BECOMES EVEN TIGHTER.

FIJI

CANADA

MATERIAL: PAPER

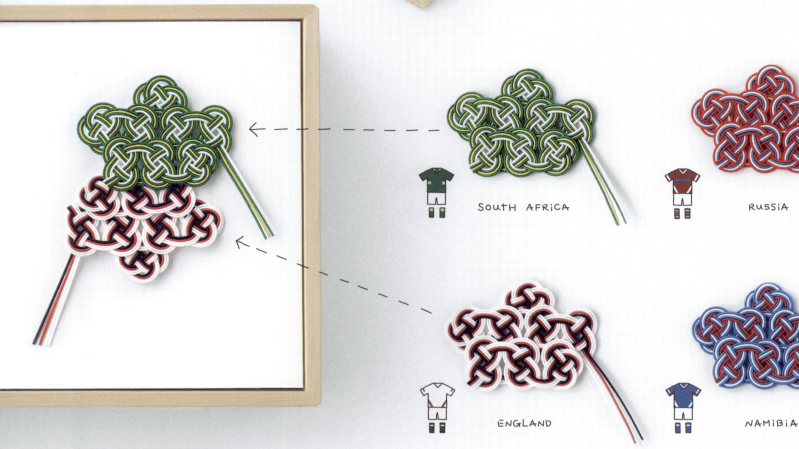

THE TWO TEAMS
IN THE FINAL

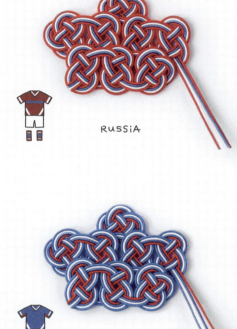

SOUTH AFRICA

RUSSIA

ENGLAND

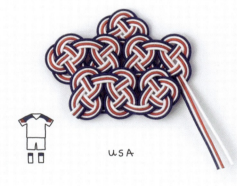

NAMIBIA

NEW ZEALAND

USA

TRADITIONAL MIZUHIKI KNOTS WERE TURNED INTO A
BROOCH THAT REPRESENTS THE POSITIONS OF RUGBY
PLAYERS IN A SCRUM. THE MIZUHIKI BROOCH
THEREBY REPRESENTS THE VALUES OF RUGBY SUCH
AS TEAMWORK AND SELF-SACRIFICE, AS WELL AS
THE JAPANESE SPIRIT OF HOSPITALITY. THE COLOURS
OF THE UNIFORMS WORN BY THE PARTICIPATING
TEAMS WERE USED, AND THE KNOTS ARE POSITIONED
TO RESEMBLE THE '3-4-1' SCRUM FORMATION.

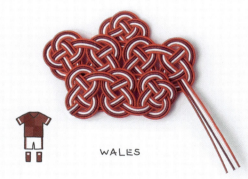

WALES

ARGENTINA

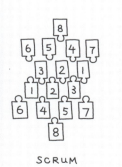
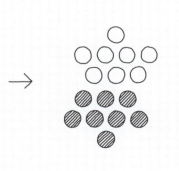

SCRUM

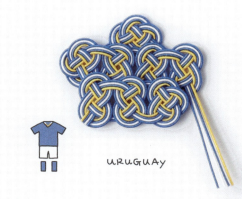

URUGUAY

GEORGIA

113

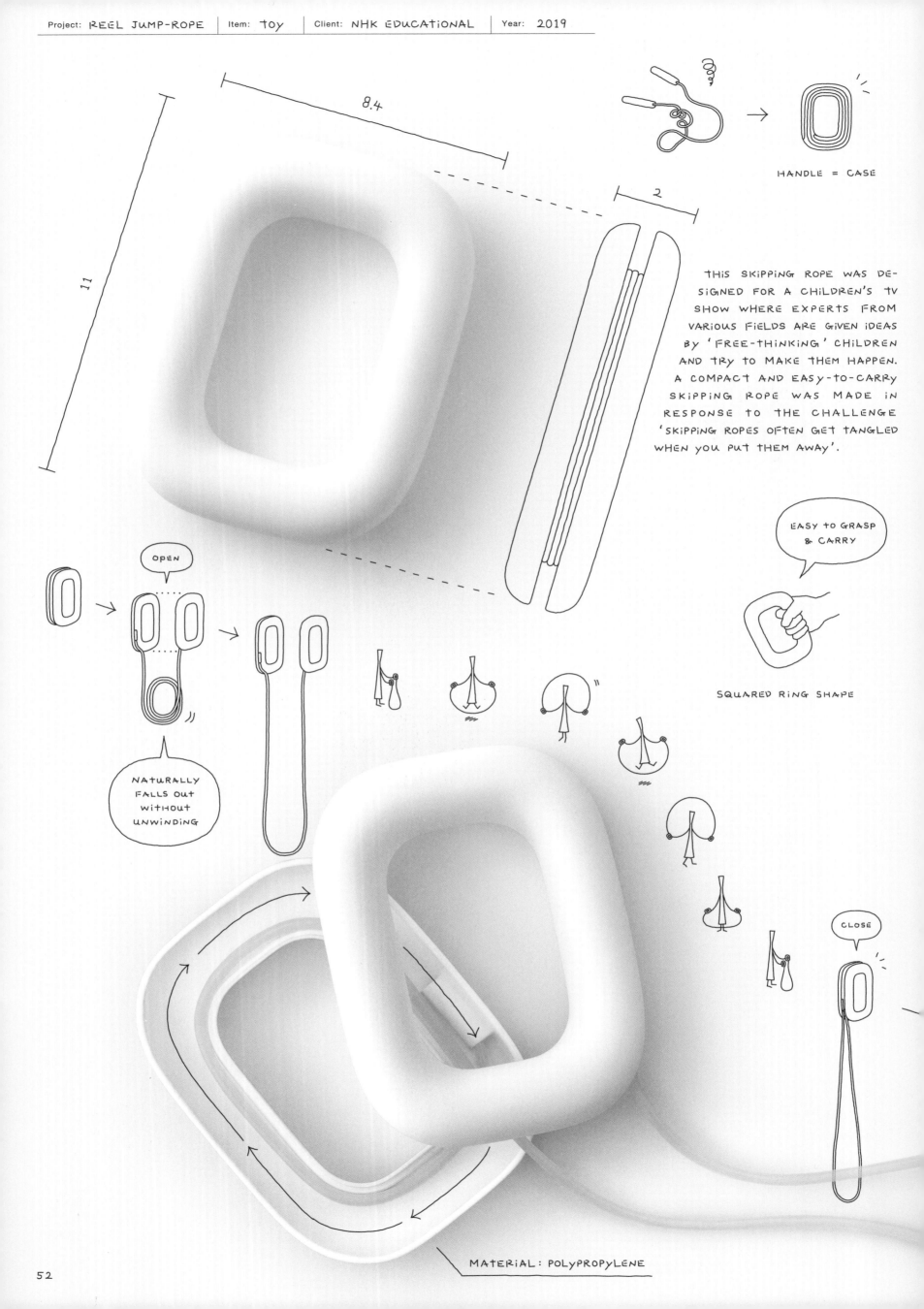

HANDLE = CASE

8.4

11

2

THIS SKIPPING ROPE WAS DE-
SIGNED FOR A CHILDREN'S TV
SHOW WHERE EXPERTS FROM
VARIOUS FIELDS ARE GIVEN IDEAS
BY 'FREE-THINKING' CHILDREN
AND TRY TO MAKE THEM HAPPEN.
A COMPACT AND EASY-TO-CARRY
SKIPPING ROPE WAS MADE IN
RESPONSE TO THE CHALLENGE
'SKIPPING ROPES OFTEN GET TANGLED
WHEN YOU PUT THEM AWAY'.

EASY TO GRASP
& CARRY

SQUARED RING SHAPE

OPEN

NATURALLY
FALLS OUT
WITHOUT
UNWINDING

CLOSE

MATERIAL: POLYPROPYLENE

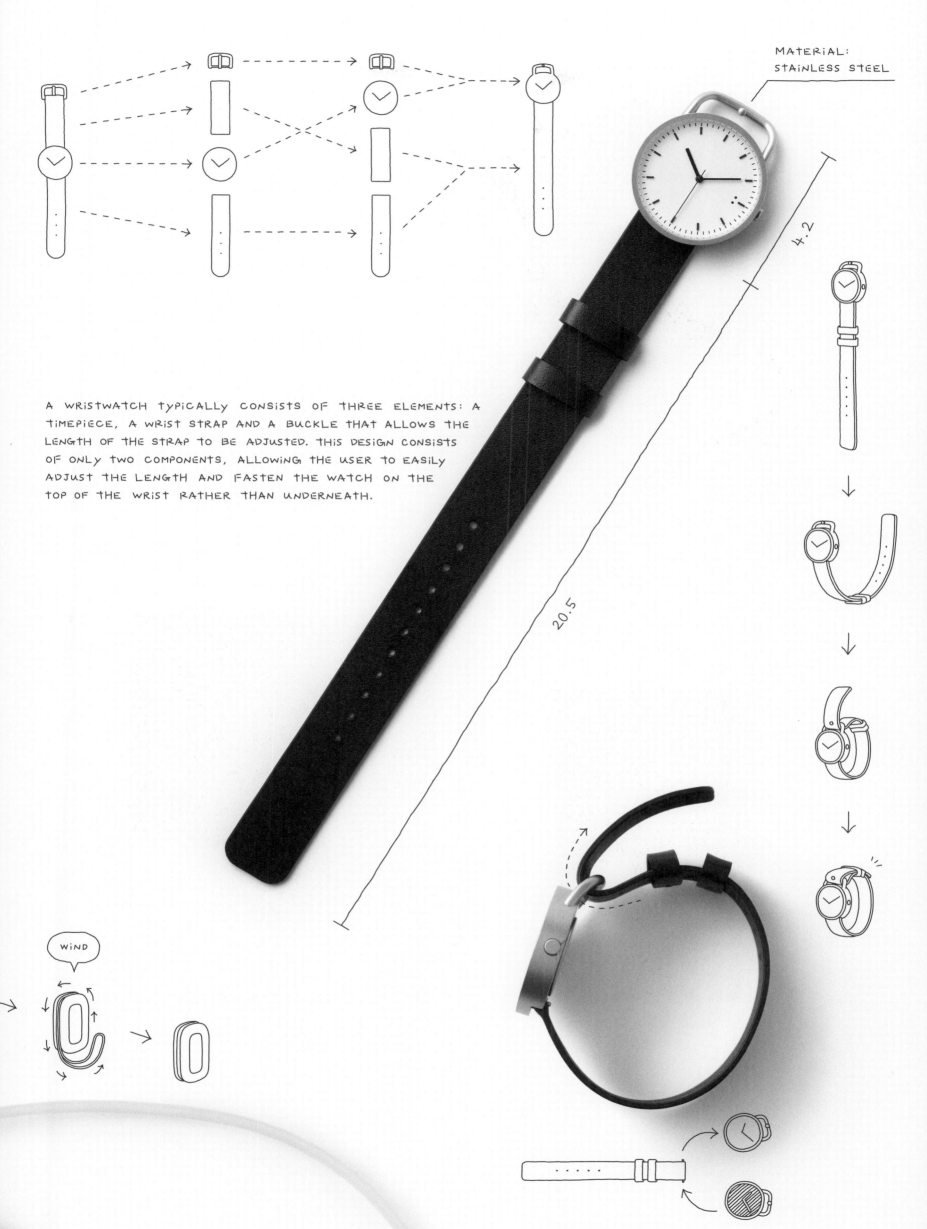

MATERIAL:
STAINLESS STEEL

4.2

20.5

A WRISTWATCH TYPICALLY CONSISTS OF THREE ELEMENTS: A
TIMEPIECE, A WRIST STRAP AND A BUCKLE THAT ALLOWS THE
LENGTH OF THE STRAP TO BE ADJUSTED. THIS DESIGN CONSISTS
OF ONLY TWO COMPONENTS, ALLOWING THE USER TO EASILY
ADJUST THE LENGTH AND FASTEN THE WATCH ON THE
TOP OF THE WRIST RATHER THAN UNDERNEATH.

WIND

EASY TO REMOVE AND REPLACE
THE STRAP AND THE TIMEPIECE

AMONG THE FOLDING SMARTPHONES WITH OLED PANEL MONITORS DEVELOPED IN RECENT YEARS, MOST FOLLOW THE TREND OF FOLDING TO THE SIZE OF A STANDARD SMARTPHONE AND UNFOLDING TO CREATE A SCREEN TWO OR THREE TIMES AS BIG. HERE, FOLDING TECHNOLOGY ENHANCES PORTABILITY, USING THE COMPACT SIZE TO CREATE A NEW SENSE OF FUNCTIONALITY INSTEAD OF ENLARGING THE SCREEN.

SLIDE

3 HINGES COVERED BY SUEDE LEATHER

SIDE BUTTON --->

THE PHONE'S SIDE BUTTONS ARE SHAPED LIKE HALF-ELLIPSES, FUNCTIONING AS TWO TO FOUR BUTTONS, BECOMING SMALL, SEMICIRCULAR BUTTONS OR COMBINING INTO ONE LARGE BUTTON AS THE FOLDING SECTIONS SLIDE UP AND DOWN.

MATERIAL:
ALUMINIUM (BODY)
SUEDE LEATHER (HINGE)

5.4

8.9

1 JUNE MON
10
09
19°

CREDIT CARD SIZE

CARD

· CLOCK
· MUSIC
· NOTIFICATION
· REMINDER
· PREVIEW

THE PHONE IN ITS FOLDED STATE IS 54MM BY 86MM, THE SIZE OF A CREDIT CARD. THE THREE HINGES FOLD IN THE SAME DIRECTION. LIKE AN INCHWORM, THE PHONE EFFECTIVELY MAKES USE OF ITS MULTIPLE JOINTS TO SLIDE SIDEWAYS, AND CAN BE TRANSFORMED BY THE USER USING ONLY ONE THUMB. THE DESIGN OPENS UP NEW POSSIBILITIES FOR SMARTPHONES, ALLOWING THEM TO BE USED NOT ONLY WHILE FULLY OPEN OR FOLDED BUT WHILE PARTIALLY UNFOLDED OR BENT.

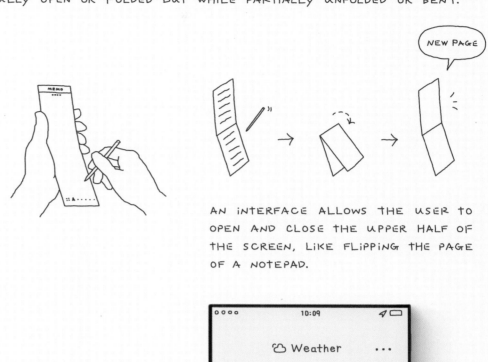

AN INTERFACE ALLOWS THE USER TO OPEN AND CLOSE THE UPPER HALF OF THE SCREEN, LIKE FLIPPING THE PAGE OF A NOTEPAD.

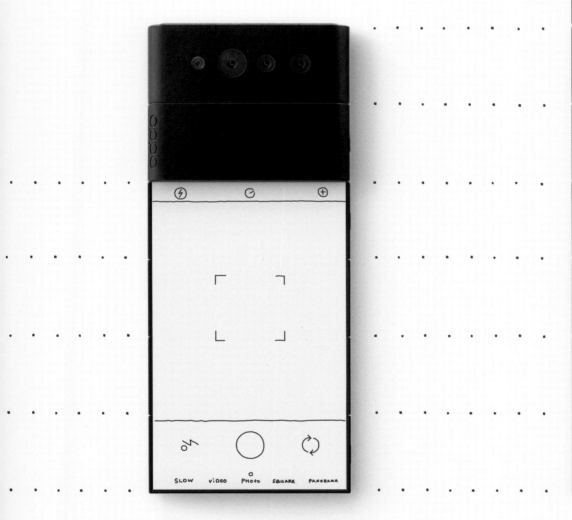

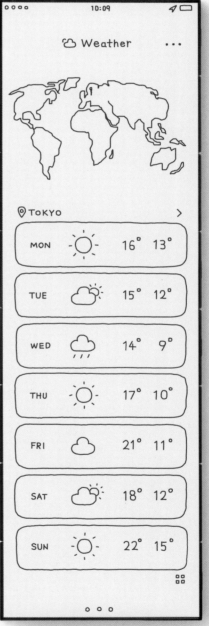

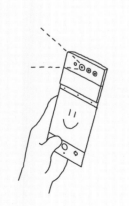

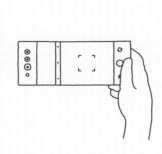

· CAMERA
· SELFIE
· CHECK THE WEB
.
.
.

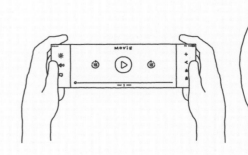

· MOVIE
· GAME
· MEMO
· MULTI-TASKING
.
.
.

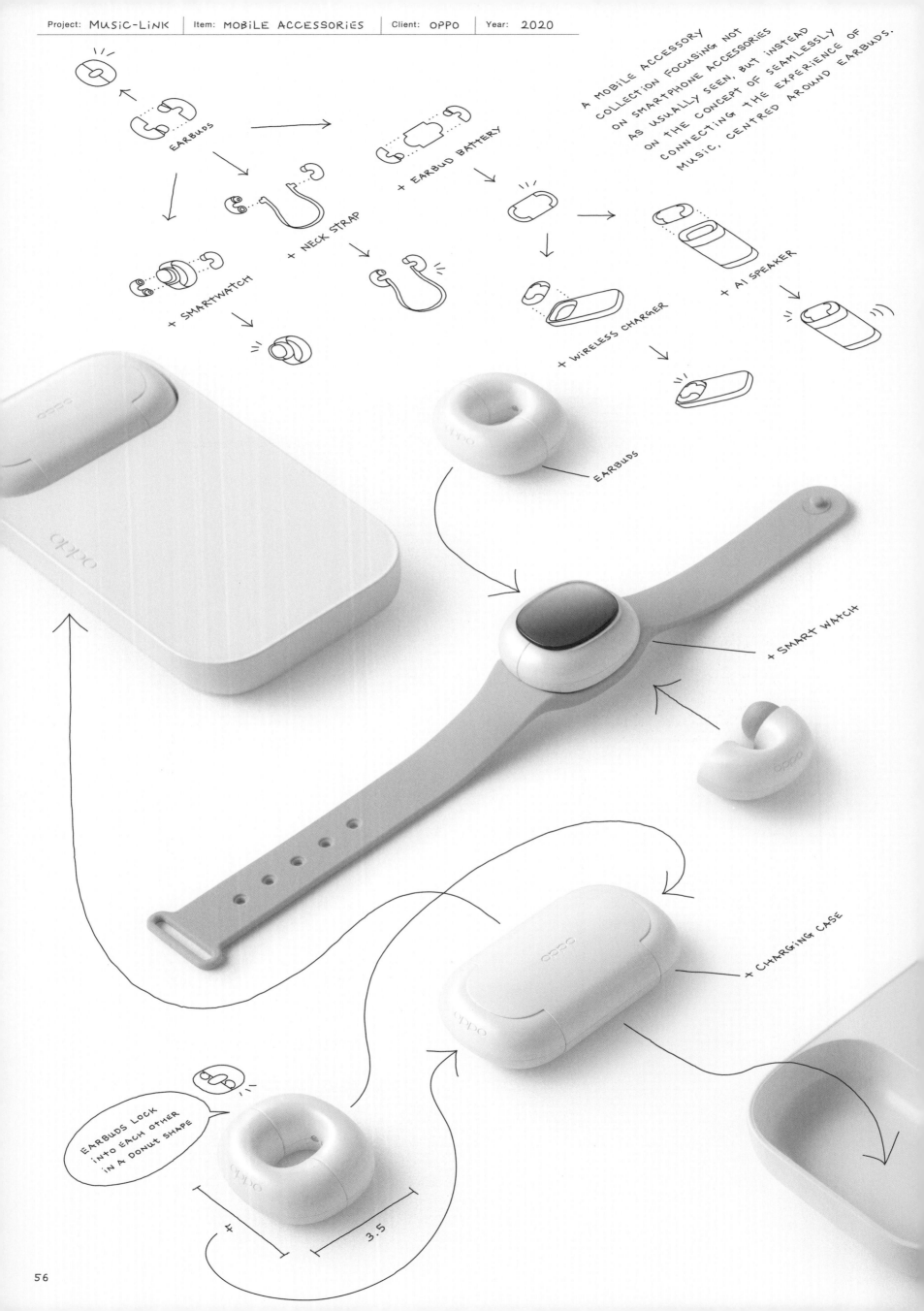

EARBUDS

+ SMARTWATCH

+ NECK STRAP

+ EARBUD BATTERY

+ WiRELESS CHARGER

+ AI SPEAKER

A MOBiLE ACCESSORY COLLECTiON FOCUSiNG NOT ON SMARTPHONE ACCESSORiES AS USUALLY SEEN, BUT INSTEAD ON THE CONCEPT OF SEAMLESSLY CONNECTiNG THE EXPERiENCE OF MUSiC, CENTRED AROUND EARBUDS.

EARBUDS

+ SMART WATCH

+ CHARGING CASE

EARBUDS LOCK iNTO EACH OTHER iN A DONUT SHAPE

4

3.5

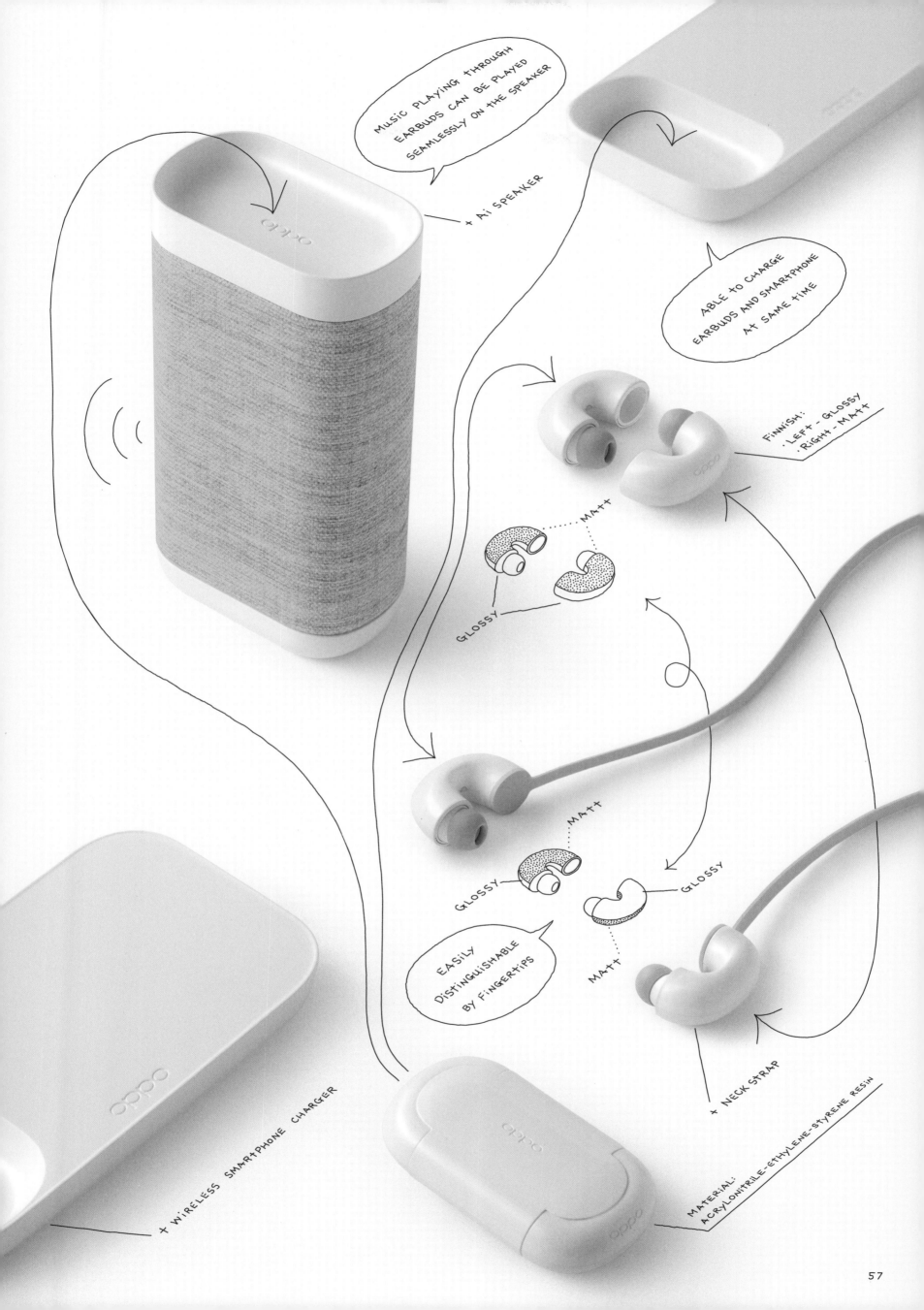

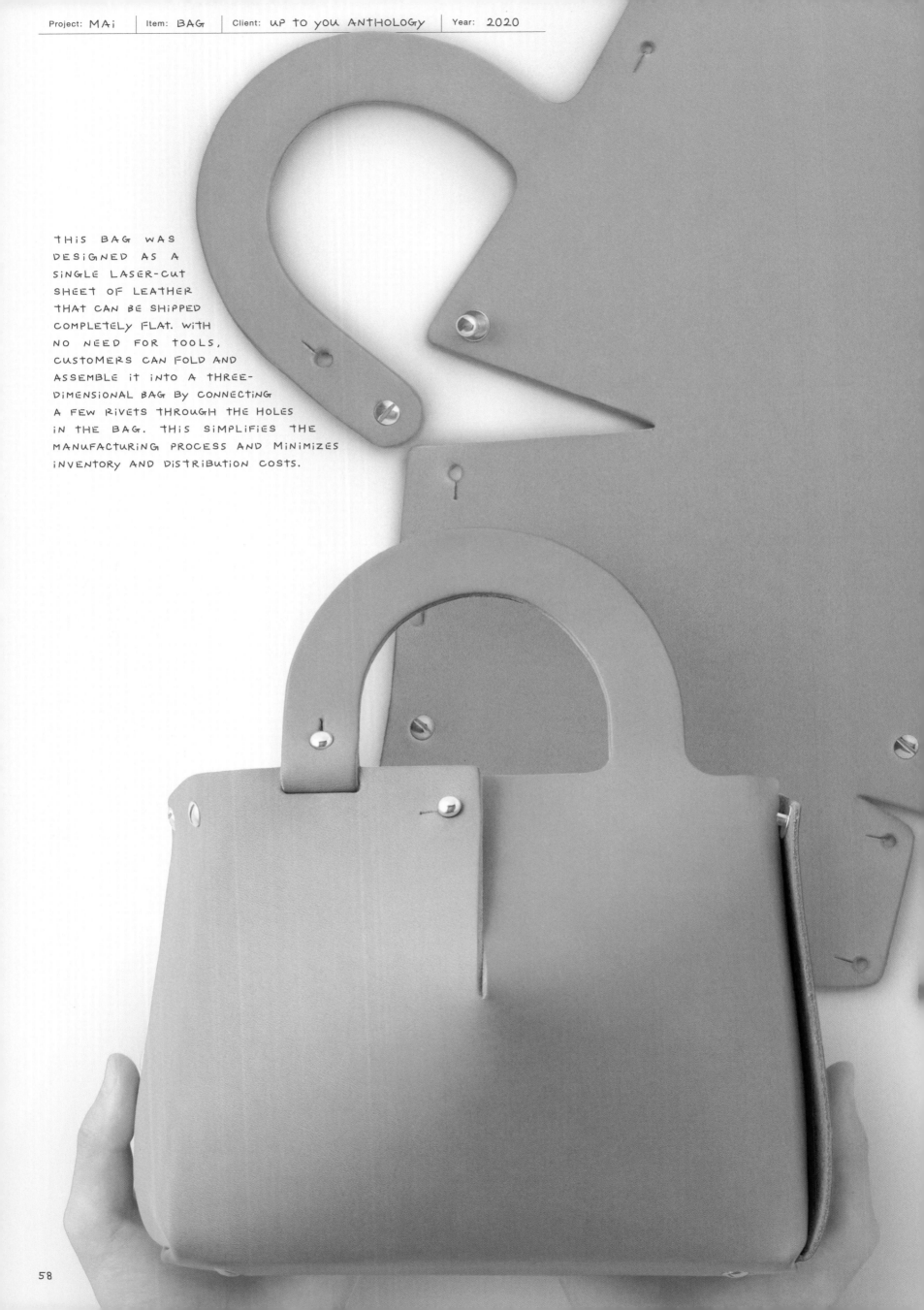

THIS BAG WAS
DESIGNED AS A
SINGLE LASER-CUT
SHEET OF LEATHER
THAT CAN BE SHIPPED
COMPLETELY FLAT. WITH
NO NEED FOR TOOLS,
CUSTOMERS CAN FOLD AND
ASSEMBLE IT INTO A THREE-
DIMENSIONAL BAG BY CONNECTING
A FEW RIVETS THROUGH THE HOLES
IN THE BAG. THIS SIMPLIFIES THE
MANUFACTURING PROCESS AND MINIMIZES
INVENTORY AND DISTRIBUTION COSTS.

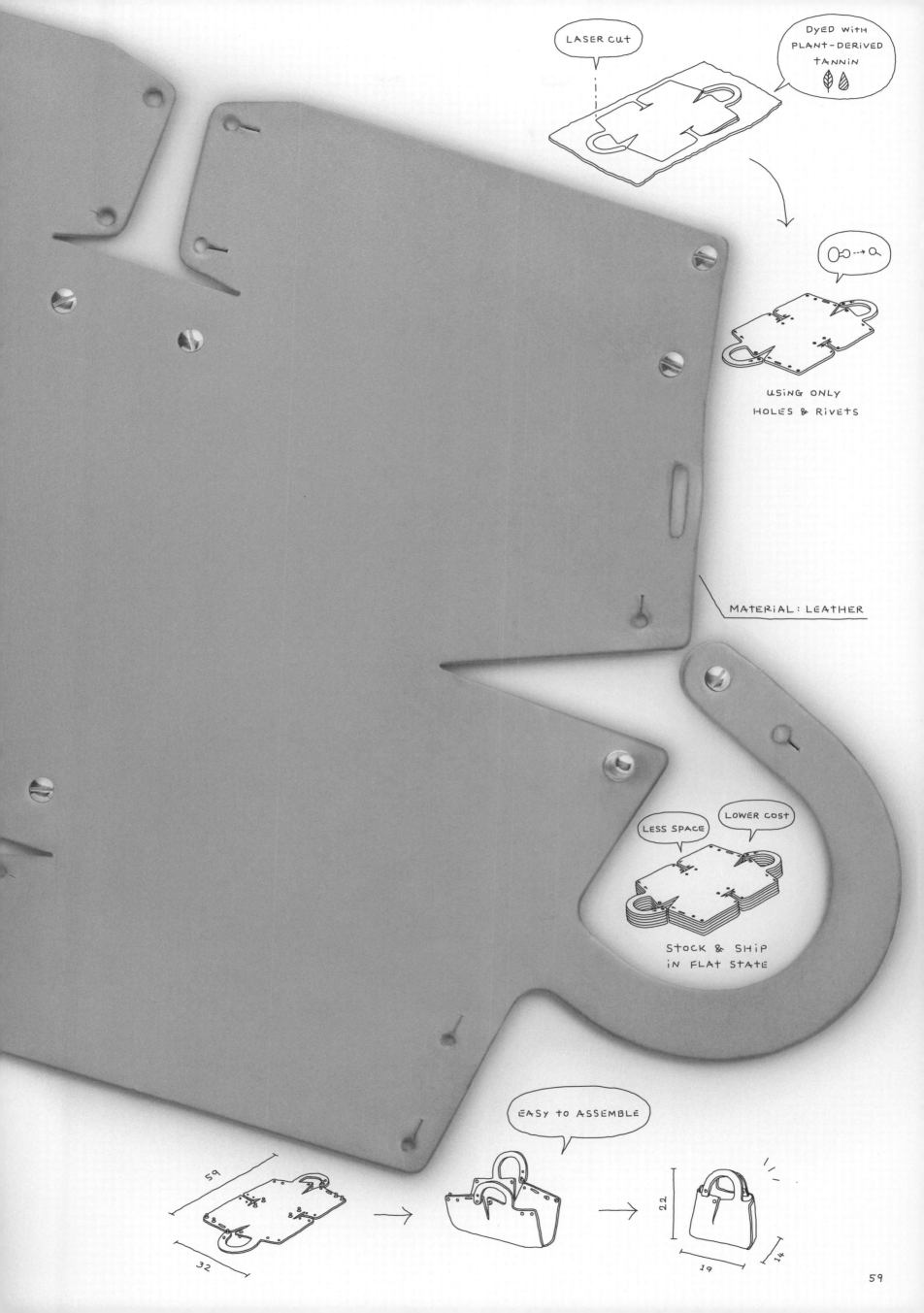

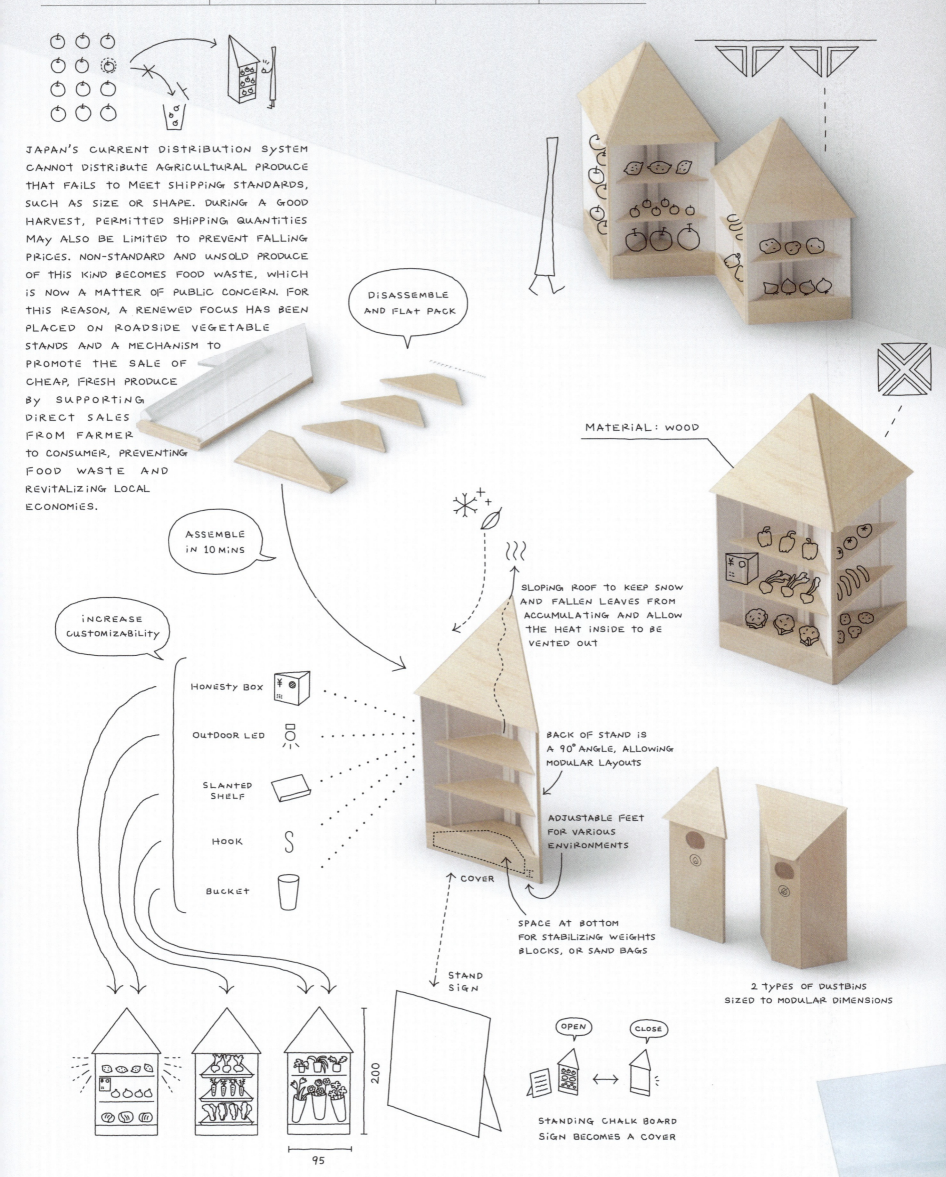

JAPAN'S CURRENT DISTRIBUTION SYSTEM CANNOT DISTRIBUTE AGRICULTURAL PRODUCE THAT FAILS TO MEET SHIPPING STANDARDS, SUCH AS SIZE OR SHAPE. DURING A GOOD HARVEST, PERMITTED SHIPPING QUANTITIES MAY ALSO BE LIMITED TO PREVENT FALLING PRICES. NON-STANDARD AND UNSOLD PRODUCE OF THIS KIND BECOMES FOOD WASTE, WHICH IS NOW A MATTER OF PUBLIC CONCERN. FOR THIS REASON, A RENEWED FOCUS HAS BEEN PLACED ON ROADSIDE VEGETABLE STANDS AND A MECHANISM TO PROMOTE THE SALE OF CHEAP, FRESH PRODUCE BY SUPPORTING DIRECT SALES FROM FARMER TO CONSUMER, PREVENTING FOOD WASTE AND REVITALIZING LOCAL ECONOMIES.

DISASSEMBLE AND FLAT PACK

ASSEMBLE IN 10 MINS

INCREASE CUSTOMIZABILITY

MATERIAL: WOOD

SLOPING ROOF TO KEEP SNOW AND FALLEN LEAVES FROM ACCUMULATING AND ALLOW THE HEAT INSIDE TO BE VENTED OUT

HONESTY BOX

OUTDOOR LED

SLANTED SHELF

HOOK

BUCKET

BACK OF STAND IS A 90° ANGLE, ALLOWING MODULAR LAYOUTS

ADJUSTABLE FEET FOR VARIOUS ENVIRONMENTS

COVER

SPACE AT BOTTOM FOR STABILIZING WEIGHTS BLOCKS, OR SAND BAGS

STAND SIGN

2 TYPES OF DUSTBINS SIZED TO MODULAR DIMENSIONS

200

95

OPEN   CLOSE

STANDING CHALK BOARD SIGN BECOMES A COVER

THE MAIN STRUCTURE COMES IN THREE SIZES: S, M, AND L. THE MEDIUM (M) VERSION IS DESIGNED WITH COMPONENTS AND PARTS FOUND AT ORDINARY HARDWARE STORES IN MIND. ONLINE AVAILABILITY OF DIAGRAMS AND ASSEMBLY GUIDES IS BEING CONSIDERED, SO IN THE FUTURE ANYONE CAN READILY DOWNLOAD THE SPECIFICATIONS, PURCHASE NECESSARY PARTS, AND ASSEMBLE THEIR OWN STANDS, THEREBY GIVING THE PROJECT GREATER POTENTIAL.

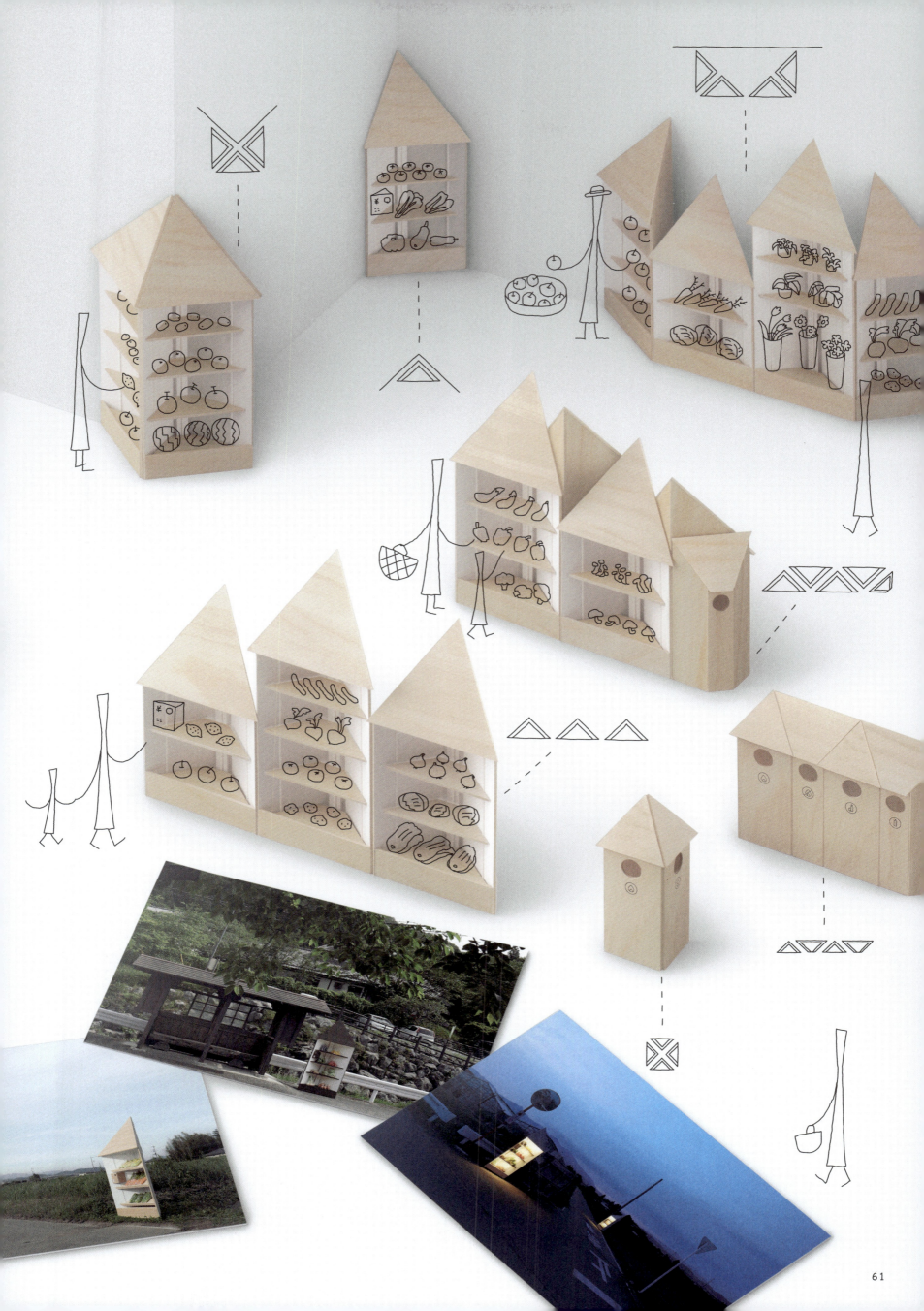

1.3

PRINCIPLE OF LEVERAGE

2.4

THE ASYMMETRICAL SHAPE ALLOWS THE KEY'S TOP AND BOTTOM TO BE EASILY IDENTIFIED, SO USERS WITH LOW VISION CAN FEEL THE CORRECT ORIENTATION IN THEIR POCKETS OR IN UNLIT AREAS WITH ONLY THEIR FINGERTIPS.

V.S

BECAUSE THE BOW OF THE KEY IS L-SHAPED, THE PRINCIPLE OF LEVERAGE ENABLES THE USER TO TURN THE KEY EFFORTLESSLY, LIKE A HEX KEY. THE DESIGN DOES NOT ADD ANY ELEMENTS TO A STANDARD KEY BUT INSTEAD STRUCTURALLY SHIFTS THE BOW OFF-CENTRE, SO THE KEY IS NEITHER WIDER NOR BULKIER THAN USUAL.

MATERIAL: BRASS ------ · HIGH DURABILITY
· RESISTANCE TO BACTERIA & VIRUSES

THiS PORTABLE PiLL CASE iS SHAPED LiKE A DOUGHNUT AND DiSPENSES PiLLS iNTO THE CENTRAL HOLE. THE RESULTiNG DESiGN iS REASSURiNG: MORE THAN ONE DOSE CANNOT COME OUT, AND THE PiLLS WiLL NOT TUMBLE OUT OF THE HAND BECAUSE OF THE PROTECTIVE BARRiER PROViDED BY THE CASE iTSELF.

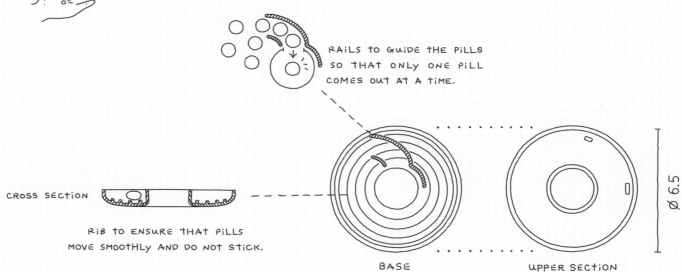

RAiLS TO GUiDE THE PiLLS SO THAT ONLY ONE PiLL COMES OUT AT A TiME.

CROSS SECTiON

RiB TO ENSURE THAT PiLLS MOVE SMOOTHLY AND DO NOT STiCK.

∅ 6.5

BASE

UPPER SECTiON

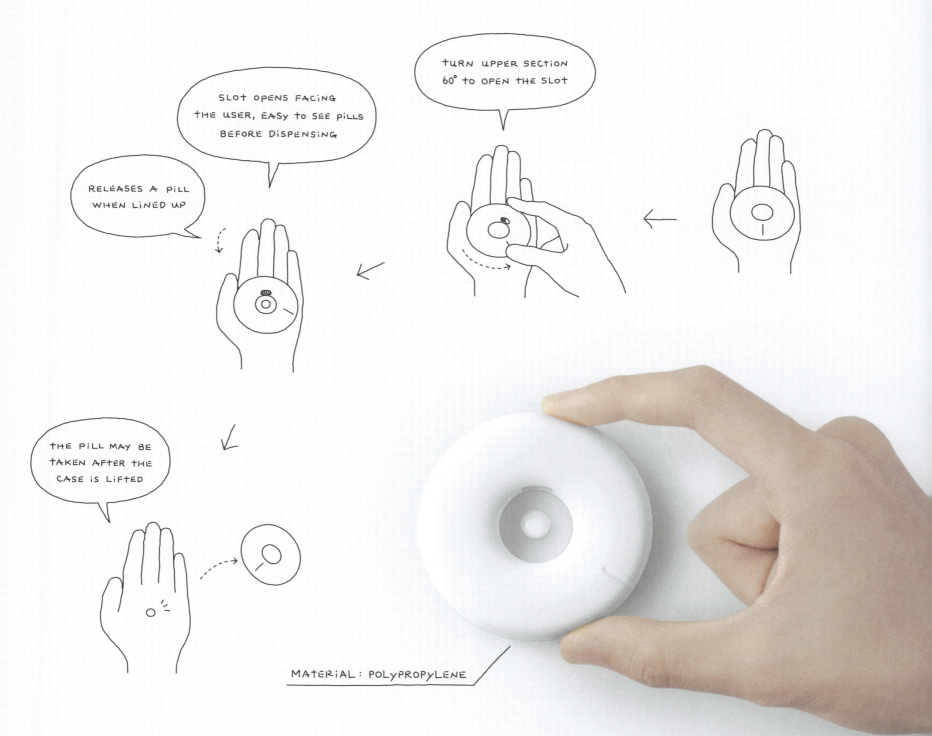

TURN UPPER SECTiON 60° TO OPEN THE SLOT

SLOT OPENS FACiNG THE USER, EASY TO SEE PiLLS BEFORE DiSPENSiNG

RELEASES A PiLL WHEN LiNED UP

THE PiLL MAY BE TAKEN AFTER THE CASE iS LiFTED

MATERiAL: POLYPROPYLENE

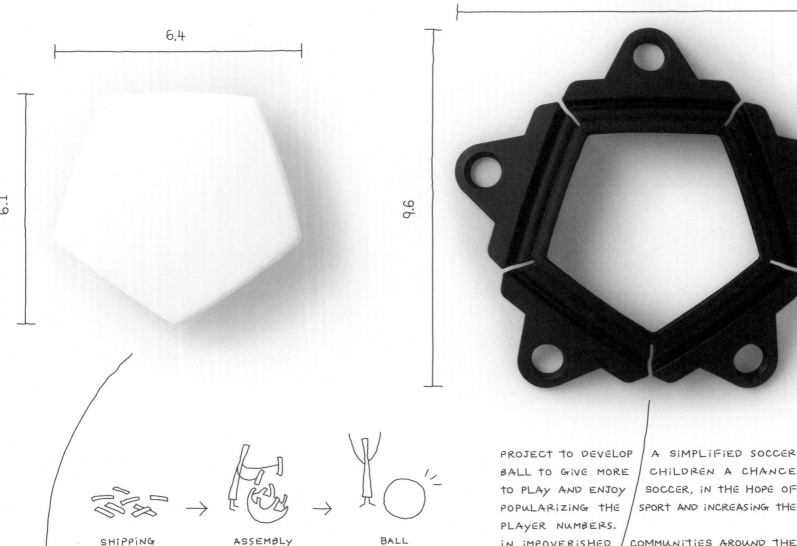

6.4

6.1

10.2

9.6

SHIPPING → ASSEMBLY → BALL

PROJECT TO DEVELOP A SIMPLIFIED SOCCER BALL TO GIVE MORE CHILDREN A CHANCE TO PLAY AND ENJOY SOCCER, IN THE HOPE OF POPULARIZING THE SPORT AND INCREASING THE PLAYER NUMBERS.

IN IMPOVERISHED COMMUNITIES AROUND THE WORLD, REGULAR SOCCER BALLS MAY BE HARD TO OBTAIN AND EVEN WHEN AVAILABLE, MAINTENANCE PRESENTS A BARRIER, EITHER BECAUSE OF THE LACK OF AIR PUMPS OR THE DETERIORA-TION AND DAMAGE OF THE TUBE INSIDE THE BALL. AS AN ANSWER TO THIS PROBLEM, A NONINFLATABLE SOCCER BALL THAT FEELS THE SAME AS KICKING AS A STANDARD BALL WAS DEVISED. ITS DESIGN WAS INSPIRED BY THE STRUCTURE OF TRADITIONAL JAPANESE WOVEN BAMBOO BALLS.

SPARE PARTS

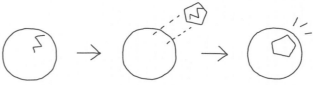

NO INFLATION NEEDED

IF A COMPONENT COMES OFF DURING PLAY, THE INTERLOCKING STRUCTURE ENSURES THE BALL WILL NOT FALL APART. THE BALL IS EASY TO MAINTAIN AND ECONOMIC IN THAT IT CAN BE REPAIRED BY REPLACING ONLY THE BROKEN COMPONENTS, CREATING LONG DURATION OF USE.

2

15

SAME WEIGHT

12 BALLS

20 BALLS

=

COMPONENTS CAN BE SHIPPED IN A
DISASSEMBLED STATE IN COMPACT
PACKAGES, POTENTIALLY CUTTING
SHIPPING COSTS.

MATERIAL:
RECYCLED POLYPROPYLENE
AND ELASTOMERIC SYNTHETIC RESIN

THE SOFT, RECYCLED POLYPROPYLENE
AND ELASTOMERIC SYNTHETIC RESIN
COMPONENTS WON'T HURT BARE FEET
AND, EVEN IF BROKEN, ARE UNLIKELY
TO DEVELOP SHARP EDGES THAT MIGHT
CAUSE INJURIES.

FUN TO
ASSEMBLE

THE AVAILABILITY OF MULTIPLE COLOURS FOR
THE SAME COMPONENTS HELPS CHILDREN
TO STRENGTHEN THEIR ATTACHMENT
TO THE BALL BY CHOOSING THEIR OWN
COLOUR SCHEME, LEADING TO A
GREATER APPRECIATION OF PLAY.

CUSTOMIZING
&
SPONSORSHIP

WITH POTENTIAL FOR PRINTING
ORIGINAL LOGOS OR DEVELOPING
BRAND-SPECIFIC COLOUR SCHEMES,
THE BUSINESS MODEL ALLOWS
COMPANIES AND ORGANIZATIONS TO
CONTRIBUTE TO VARIOUS EDUCATIONAL
INSTITUTIONS AND CLUB TEAMS.

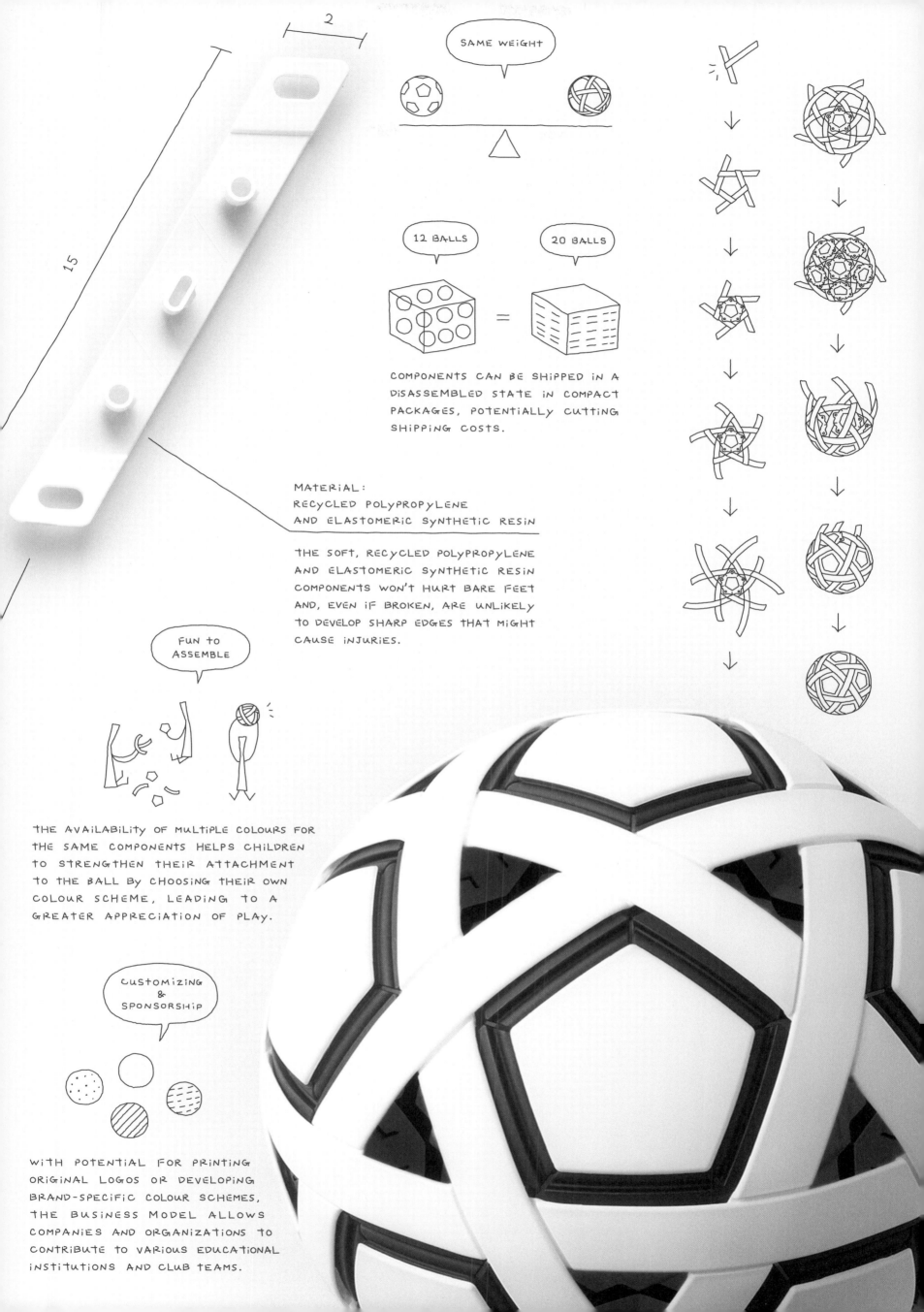

A BUDDHIST ALTAR SET, DESIGNED TO FIT SHIFTING JAPANESE ATTITUDES TO LIFE, DEATH AND COMMEMORATION. WHETHER DUE TO THE ECONOMY OR THE DECLINING BIRTHRATE AND AGING POPULATION, AN INCREASING NUMBER OF HOUSEHOLDS ARE FINDING IT HARD TO BUILD AND MAINTAIN GRAVESITES ON LAND MEANT FOR PASSING ON TO FUTURE GENERATIONS. MOREOVER, THE DIVERSIFICATION OF JAPANESE VIEWS ON LIFE AND DEATH IS ERODING THE DESIRE TO INTER ASHES AT BUDDHIST TEMPLES AND PLACE TRADITIONAL ALTARS WITHIN HOMES. MEANWHILE, MEMORIAL JEWELRY AND URNS DESIGNED FOR INTERIOR SPACES ARE GAINING POPULARITY, WITH THEIR AIM OF FOCUSING ON EMOTIONAL VALUES AND ALLEVIATING A MOURNER'S SENSE OF LOSS AND LONELINESS BY INCORPORATING THE DECEASED'S ASHES INTO EVERYDAY LIFE. THE FREE-SPIRITED APPROACH OF RETURNING LOVED ONES TO NATURE, THROUGH A TREE BURIAL OR BY SCATTERING POWDERED BONES IN THE SEA, IS ALSO GAINING TRACTION. IT IS AGAINST SUCH A BACKDROP THAT THIS BUDDHIST ALTAR WAS DESIGNED. COMPRISING FOUR ELEMENTS — URN, INCENSE BURNER, VASE AND BELL — THE ALTAR SUBTLY INTEGRATES THE ROLES OF ALL FOUR INTO A SINGLE LANDSCAPE, RATHER THAN MERELY PROVIDING A TRAY ON WHICH THE COMPONENT ELEMENTS ARE ARRANGED.

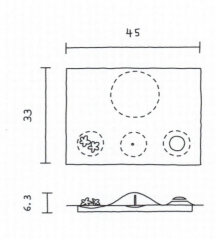

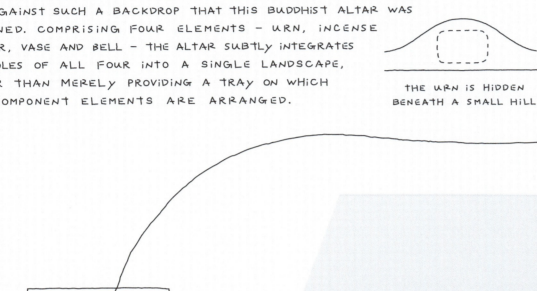

THE URN IS HIDDEN BENEATH A SMALL HILL

URN

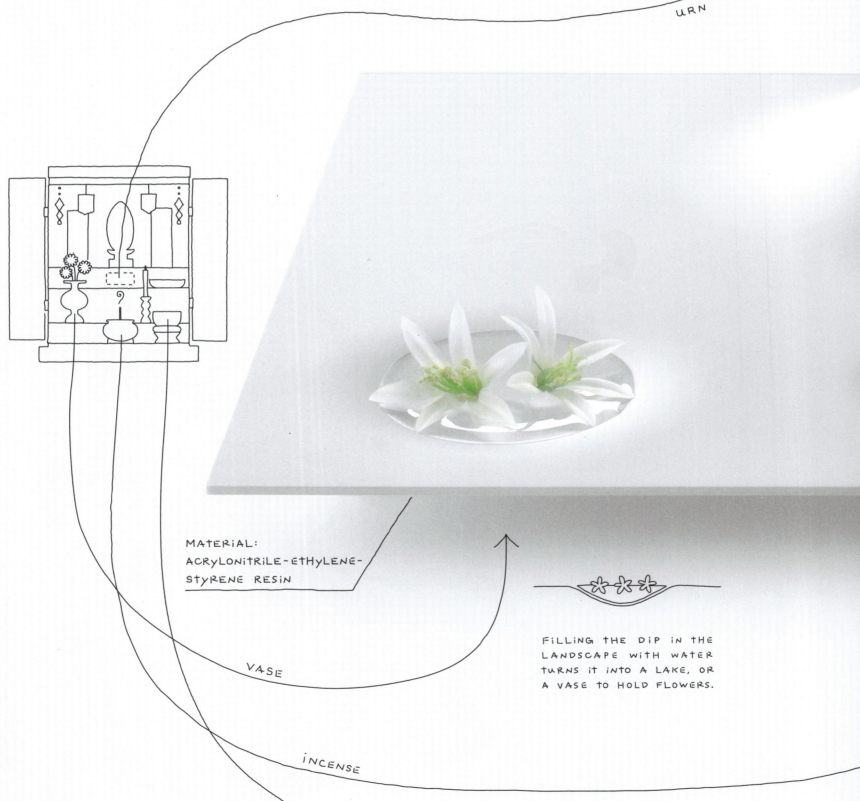

MATERIAL:
ACRYLONITRILE-ETHYLENE-STYRENE RESIN

VASE

FILLING THE DIP IN THE LANDSCAPE WITH WATER TURNS IT INTO A LAKE, OR A VASE TO HOLD FLOWERS.

INCENSE

BELL

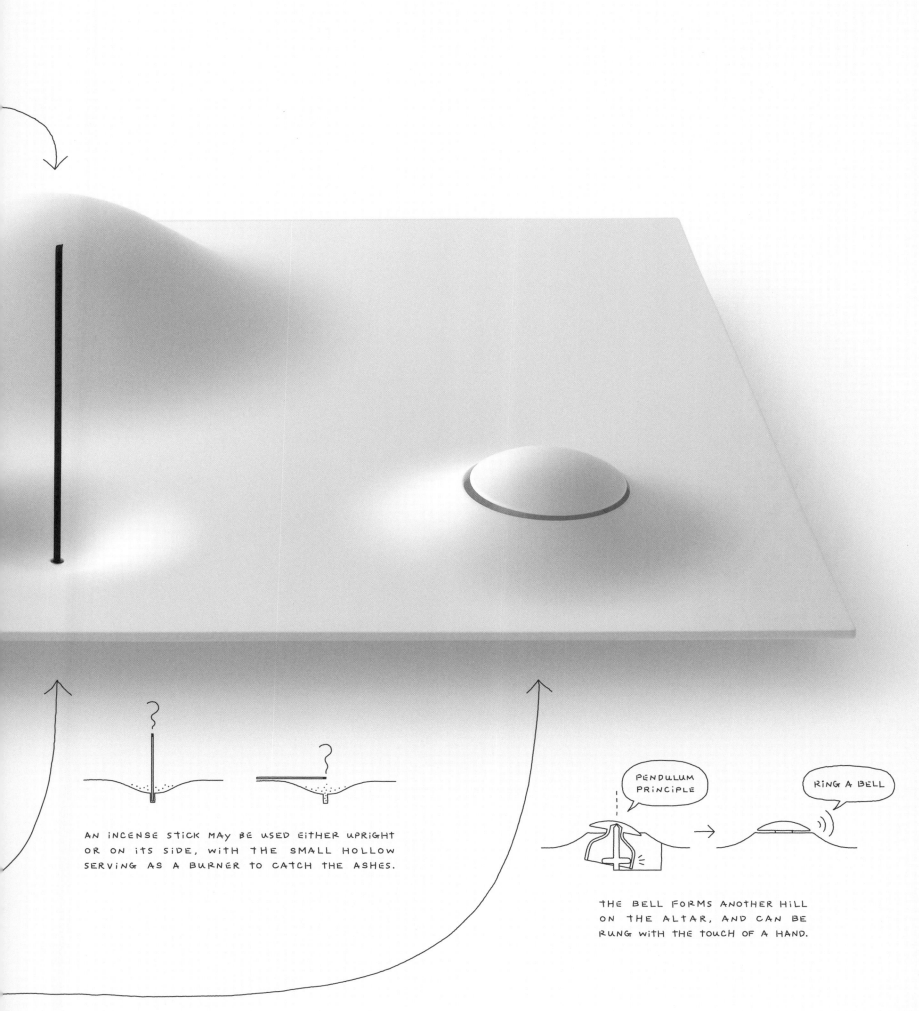

AN INCENSE STICK MAY BE USED EITHER UPRIGHT
OR ON ITS SIDE, WITH THE SMALL HOLLOW
SERVING AS A BURNER TO CATCH THE ASHES.

PENDULUM
PRINCIPLE

RING A BELL

THE BELL FORMS ANOTHER HILL
ON THE ALTAR, AND CAN BE
RUNG WITH THE TOUCH OF A HAND.

AN EXTRUDED ALUMINIUM BAR
IN THE FORM OF THE LOGO

'大' IS PART OF
THE KANJI
CHARACTER FOR
'UNIVERSITY',

'MIND'   'TECHNIQUE'

'VIRTUE'

'KNOWLEDGE'   'PHYSICAL
STRENGTH'

UNIVAS

THE LOGO WAS DESIGNED TO
CONVEY MULTIPLE MESSAGES,
BRINGING TOGETHER JAPANESE
AND WESTERN CULTURES
TRADITION AND YOUTHFULNESS.

TROPHY

SILVER   GOLD   BRONZE

30
21

UNIVAS (JAPAN ASSOCIATION FOR UNIVERSITY ATHLETICS AND SPORT) WAS ESTABLISHED TO TAKE A SUPERVISORY AND PROMOTIONAL ROLE OVER COLLEGE SPORTS IN JAPAN. IT OFFERS A BROAD RANGE OF SUPPORT TO STUDENTS, UNIVERSITIES AND SPORTS ASSOCIATIONS, FROM ORGANIZING EVENTS AND AWARDING ATHLETES, TO SETTING RULES, STAGING PR ACTIVITIES, MANAGING SPORTS FACILITIES, AND TRAINING COACHES.
THE TROPHIES AND MEDALS GIVEN AT THE AWARD CEREMONY ARE CUT FROM AN EXTRUDED BAR OF ALUMINIUM IN THE SHAPE OF THE UNIVAS LOGO.

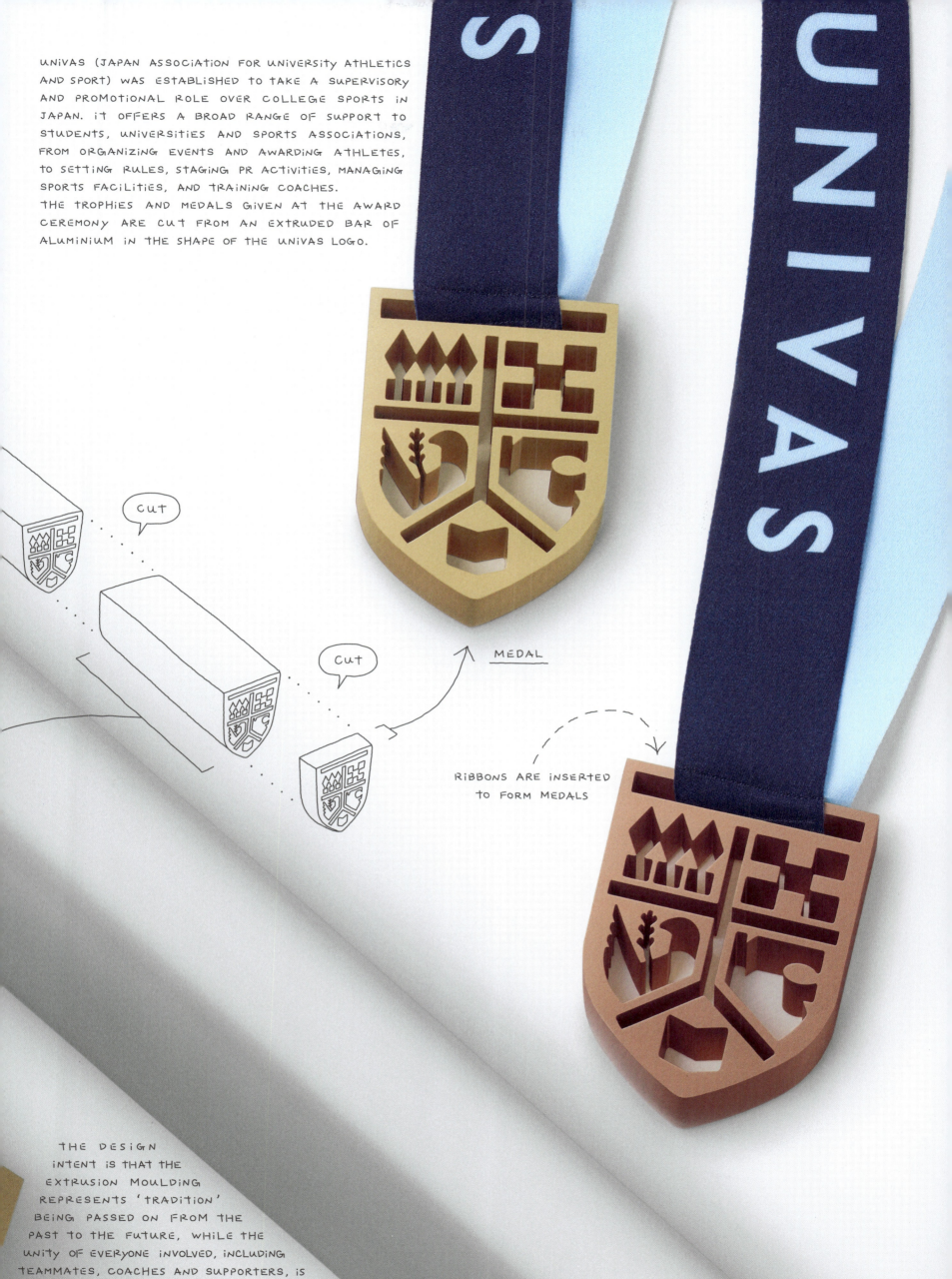

CUT

CUT

MEDAL

RIBBONS ARE INSERTED TO FORM MEDALS

THE DESIGN INTENT IS THAT THE EXTRUSION MOULDING REPRESENTS 'TRADITION' BEING PASSED ON FROM THE PAST TO THE FUTURE, WHILE THE UNITY OF EVERYONE INVOLVED, INCLUDING TEAMMATES, COACHES AND SUPPORTERS, IS REPRESENTED BY USING A SINGLE DESIGN FOR ALL THE AWARDS.

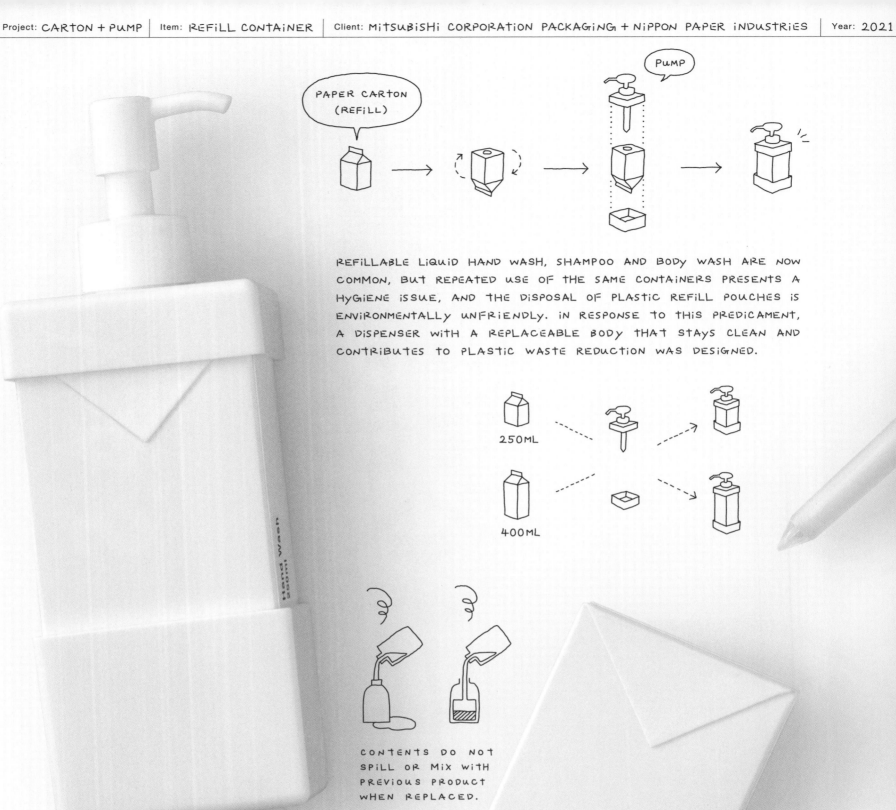

PAPER CARTON (REFILL)

PUMP

REFILLABLE LIQUID HAND WASH, SHAMPOO AND BODY WASH ARE NOW COMMON, BUT REPEATED USE OF THE SAME CONTAINERS PRESENTS A HYGIENE ISSUE, AND THE DISPOSAL OF PLASTIC REFILL POUCHES IS ENVIRONMENTALLY UNFRIENDLY. IN RESPONSE TO THIS PREDICAMENT, A DISPENSER WITH A REPLACEABLE BODY THAT STAYS CLEAN AND CONTRIBUTES TO PLASTIC WASTE REDUCTION WAS DESIGNED.

250ML

400ML

CONTENTS DO NOT SPILL OR MIX WITH PREVIOUS PRODUCT WHEN REPLACED.

RECYCLABLE

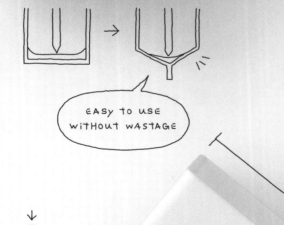

EASY TO USE WITHOUT WASTAGE

6.3

5

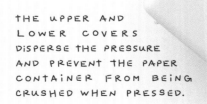

THE UPPER AND LOWER COVERS DISPERSE THE PRESSURE AND PREVENT THE PAPER CONTAINER FROM BEING CRUSHED WHEN PRESSED.

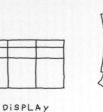

DISPLAY

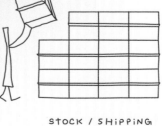

STOCK / SHIPPING

EFFICIENT USE OF SPACE

MATERIAL: POLYPROPYLENE

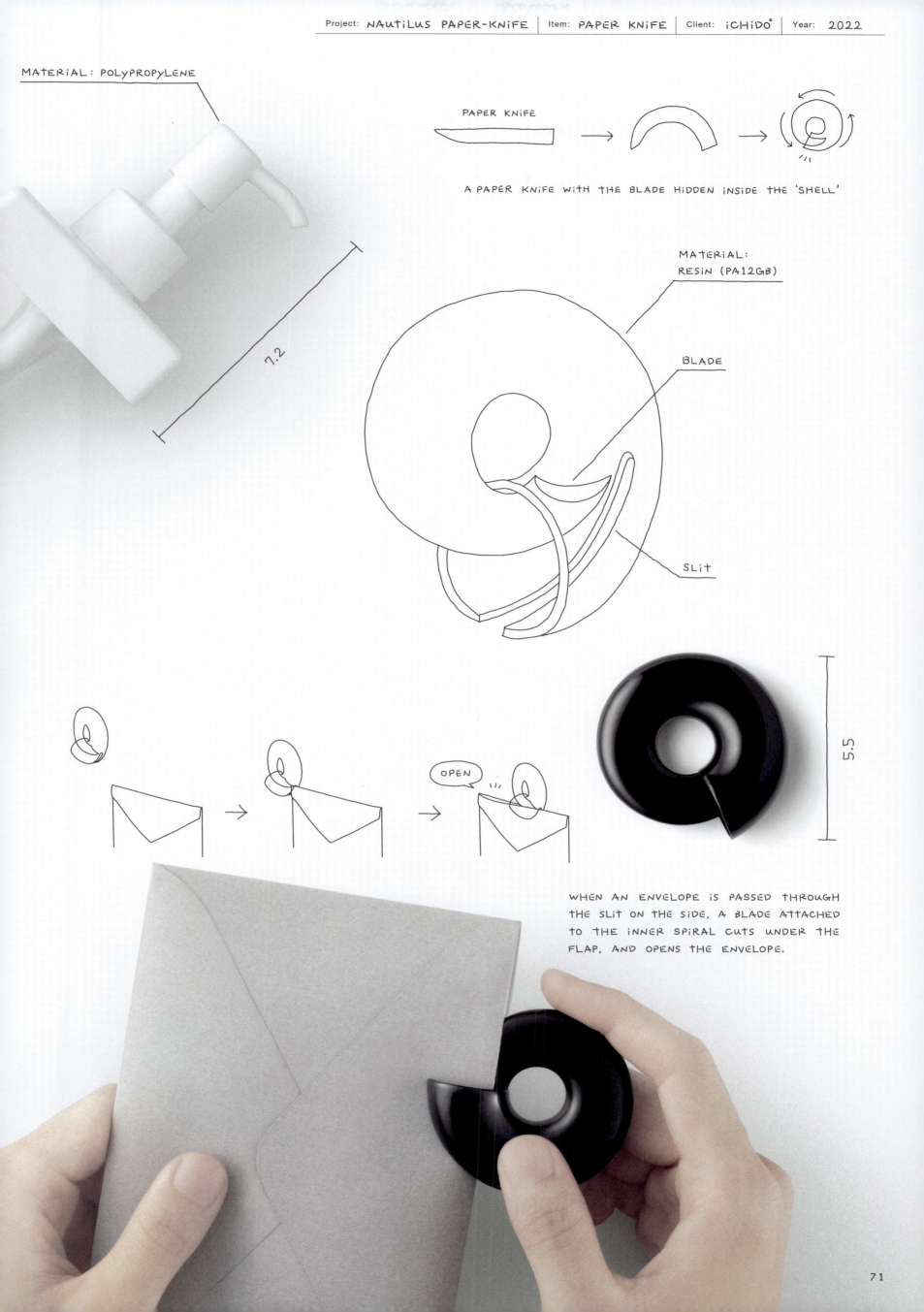

PAPER KNIFE

A PAPER KNIFE WITH THE BLADE HIDDEN INSIDE THE 'SHELL'

7.2

MATERIAL: RESIN (PA12GB)

BLADE

SLIT

5.5

OPEN

WHEN AN ENVELOPE IS PASSED THROUGH
THE SLIT ON THE SIDE, A BLADE ATTACHED
TO THE INNER SPIRAL CUTS UNDER THE
FLAP, AND OPENS THE ENVELOPE.

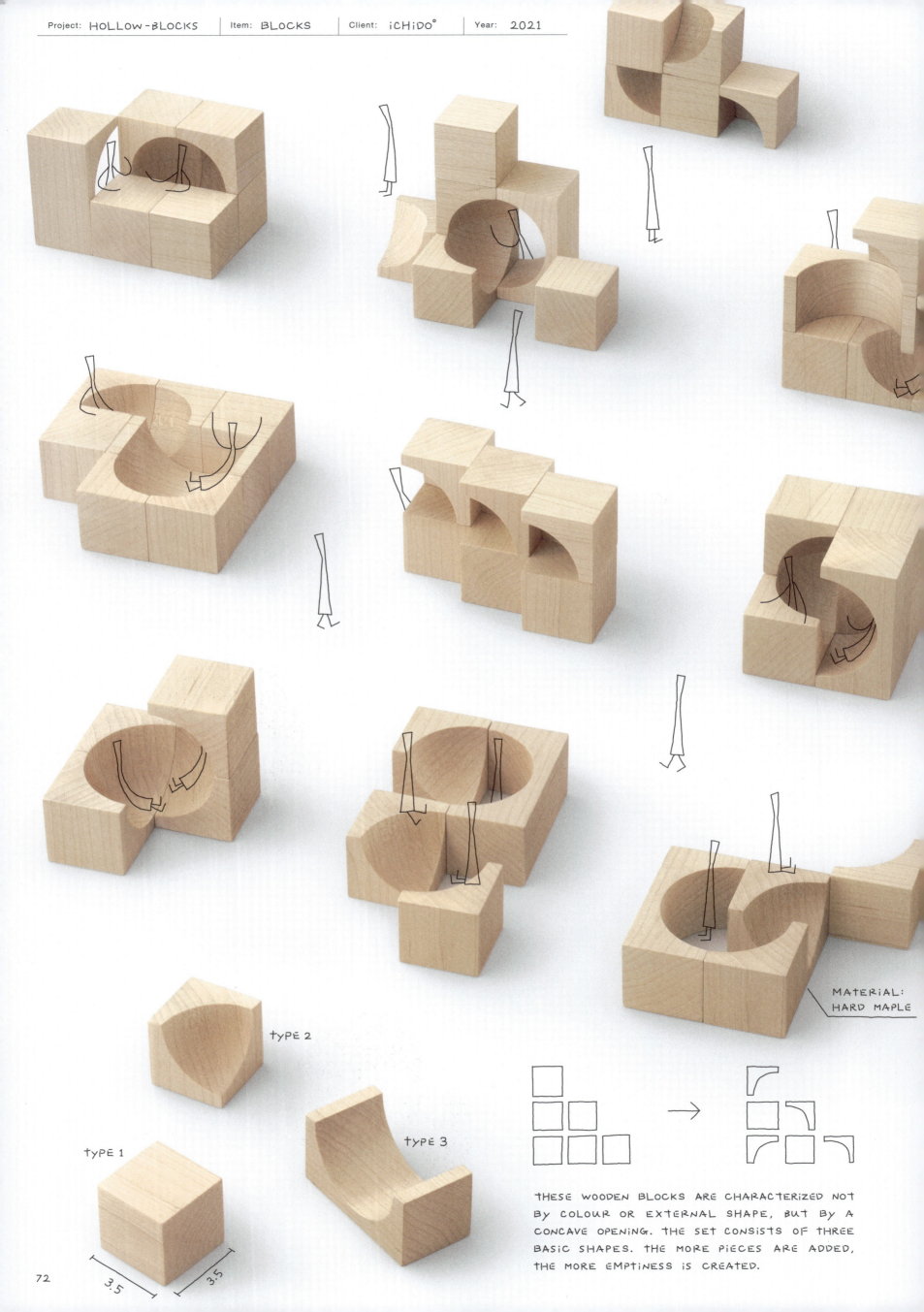

TYPE 2

TYPE 1

TYPE 3

3.5

3.5

MATERIAL:
HARD MAPLE

THESE WOODEN BLOCKS ARE CHARACTERIZED NOT
BY COLOUR OR EXTERNAL SHAPE, BUT BY A
CONCAVE OPENING. THE SET CONSISTS OF THREE
BASIC SHAPES. THE MORE PIECES ARE ADDED,
THE MORE EMPTINESS IS CREATED.

IS IT POSSIBLE TO MAKE A TOP FROM A SHAPE THAT DOESN'T LOOK LIKE IT SPINS?

STUDYING THE CONDITIONS THAT WOULD MAKE AN OBJECT SPIN CLEANLY MADE SOMETHING CLEAR: MATCHING THE AXIS ON WHICH THE OBJECT IS DESIGNED TO SPIN, AND THE AXIS ON WHICH IT WILL SPIN MOST EASILY, IS JUST AS IMPORTANT AS CONDITIONS SUCH AS ITS CENTRE OF GRAVITY, WEIGHT OR TIP SHAPE. THE AXIS ON WHICH THE OBJECT IS DESIGNED TO SPIN IS ESSENTIALLY A LINE CONNECTING THE POINT AT WHICH IT TOUCHES THE SURFACE BELOW AND THE HANDLE BY WHICH IT IS SPUN. IT IS, MORE OR LESS, THE INTERFACE THROUGH WHICH SOMEONE INTENDS TO SPIN THE OBJECT. MEANWHILE, THE AXIS ON WHICH IT WILL SPIN MOST EASILY IS ALSO CALLED THE MAJOR PRINCIPAL AXIS OF INERTIA. SUCH A STATE EXISTS FOR ANY OBJECT ANYWHERE. MAKING THESE TWO AXES ONE AND THE SAME PREVENTS IMMEDIATE WOBBLING AND ENABLES THE OBJECT TO SPIN LONGER.

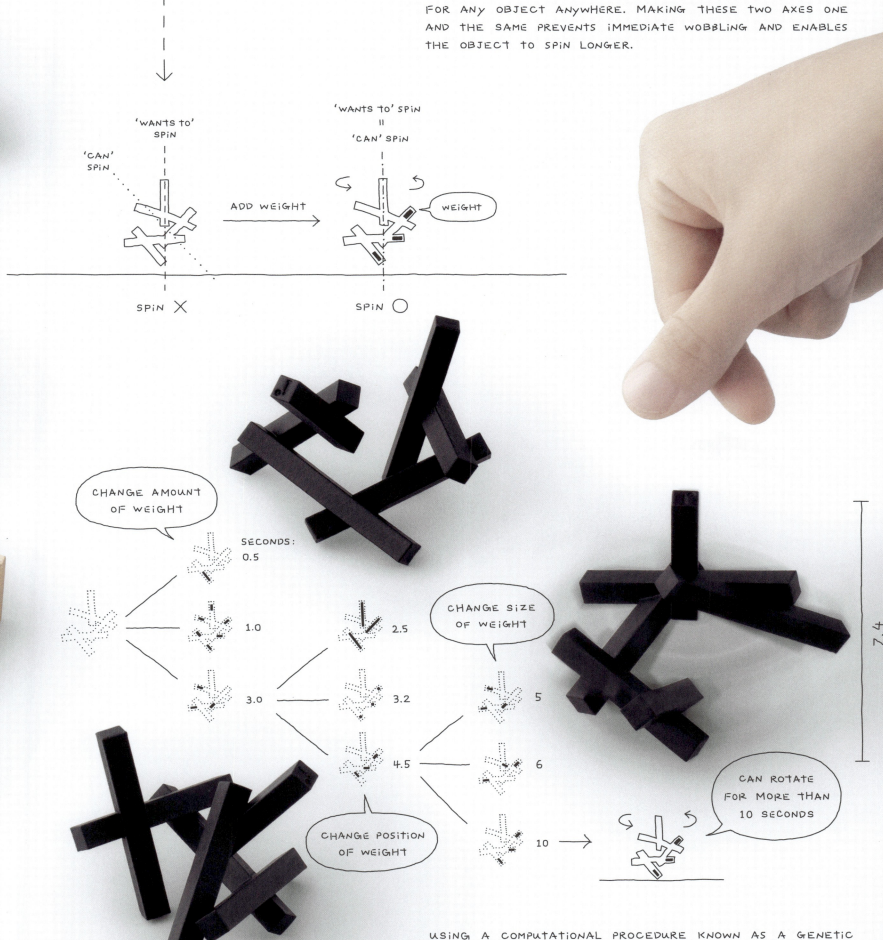

USING A COMPUTATIONAL PROCEDURE KNOWN AS A GENETIC ALGORITHM, FOUR CONDITIONS WERE EVALUATED – CENTRE OF GRAVITY, WEIGHT, TIP SHAPE, AND THE AXIS BY WHICH THE TOP IS BOTH DESIGNED TO BE SPUN AND IS EASIEST TO SPIN – IN ORDER TO FIND THE OPTIMAL COMBINATION OF THE OBJECT'S SHAPE AND THE WEIGHT'S SIZE AND POSITION.

73

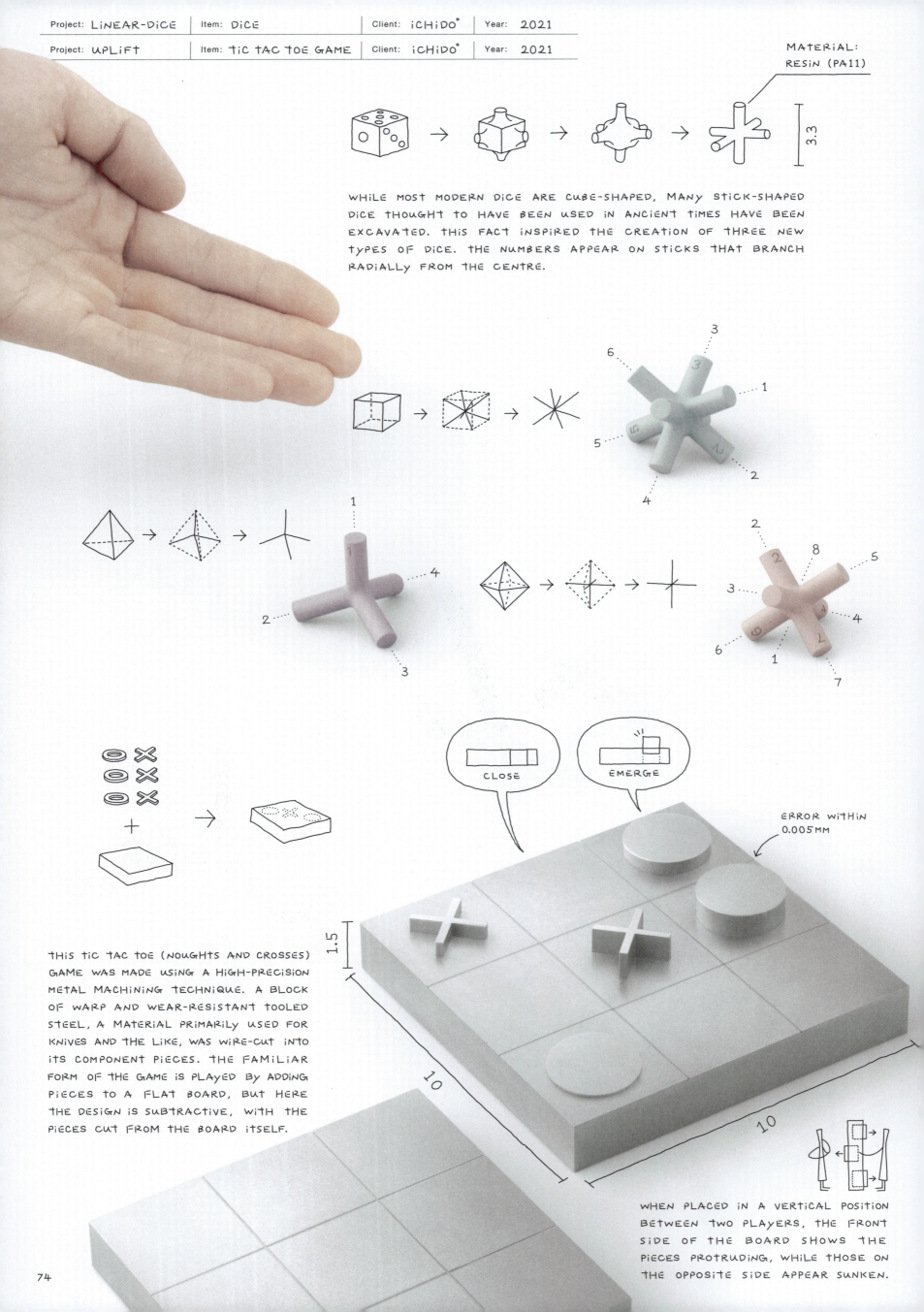

MATERIAL:
RESIN (PA11)

3.3

WHILE MOST MODERN DICE ARE CUBE-SHAPED, MANY STICK-SHAPED DICE THOUGHT TO HAVE BEEN USED IN ANCIENT TIMES HAVE BEEN EXCAVATED. THIS FACT INSPIRED THE CREATION OF THREE NEW TYPES OF DICE. THE NUMBERS APPEAR ON STICKS THAT BRANCH RADIALLY FROM THE CENTRE.

CLOSE

EMERGE

ERROR WITHIN 0.005MM

THIS TIC TAC TOE (NOUGHTS AND CROSSES) GAME WAS MADE USING A HIGH-PRECISION METAL MACHINING TECHNIQUE. A BLOCK OF WARP AND WEAR-RESISTANT TOOLED STEEL, A MATERIAL PRIMARILY USED FOR KNIVES AND THE LIKE, WAS WIRE-CUT INTO ITS COMPONENT PIECES. THE FAMILIAR FORM OF THE GAME IS PLAYED BY ADDING PIECES TO A FLAT BOARD, BUT HERE THE DESIGN IS SUBTRACTIVE, WITH THE PIECES CUT FROM THE BOARD ITSELF.

1.5

10

10

WHEN PLACED IN A VERTICAL POSITION BETWEEN TWO PLAYERS, THE FRONT SIDE OF THE BOARD SHOWS THE PIECES PROTRUDING, WHILE THOSE ON THE OPPOSITE SIDE APPEAR SUNKEN.

REFRACTiVE iNDEX OF
1.333 — 1.475

ULTRA-TRANSPARENT
SiLiCONE

=

WATER-DiLUTED
GLYCERiN

GENERALLY, WATER-DiLUTED GLYCERiN iS USED TO ALLOW THE PARTICLES iN A SNOW GLOBE TO FLUTTER AND SWiRL, WiTH A REFRACTiVE iNDEX OF APPROXiMATELY 1.333 TO 1.475. BY CREATiNG AN OBJECT USiNG AN ULTRA-TRANSPARENT SiLiCONE RESiN WiTH A REFRACTiVE iNDEX AS CLOSE AS POSSiBLE TO THiS VALUE, iTS FORMS SEEM TO DiSAPPEAR.

iNViSiBLE OBJECT

?

9.5

Ø6.5

AS THE SNOW SLOWLY ACCUMULATES, A VAGUE OUTLINE BEGiNS TO APPEAR. WHEN THE SNOW iS COMPLETELY SETTLED, THE MOTiF iS CLEARLY ViSiBLE iN WHiTE, WHiLE THE LOWER PART OF THE OBJECT WiTHOUT SNOW LOOKS LiKE iTS SHADOW.

TAKES TIME TO MAKE BOUQUET AFTER ORDERING

LOSE FRESHNESS ON DISPLAY

VASE NEEDED

IT IS COMMON FOR FLORISTS TO MAKE BOUQUETS ONLY AFTER THEY ARE ORDERED, WHICH CREATES A WAIT TIME FOR THE CUSTOMER AND MAKES IT DIFFICULT TO PICTURE WHAT THE FINAL PRODUCT WILL LOOK LIKE. BECAUSE PRE-BUNCHED FLOWERS CANNOT GET ENOUGH WATER TO STAY FRESH, IT WAS DIFFICULT TO ARRANGE PREMADE BOUQUETS ON STORE SHELVES.

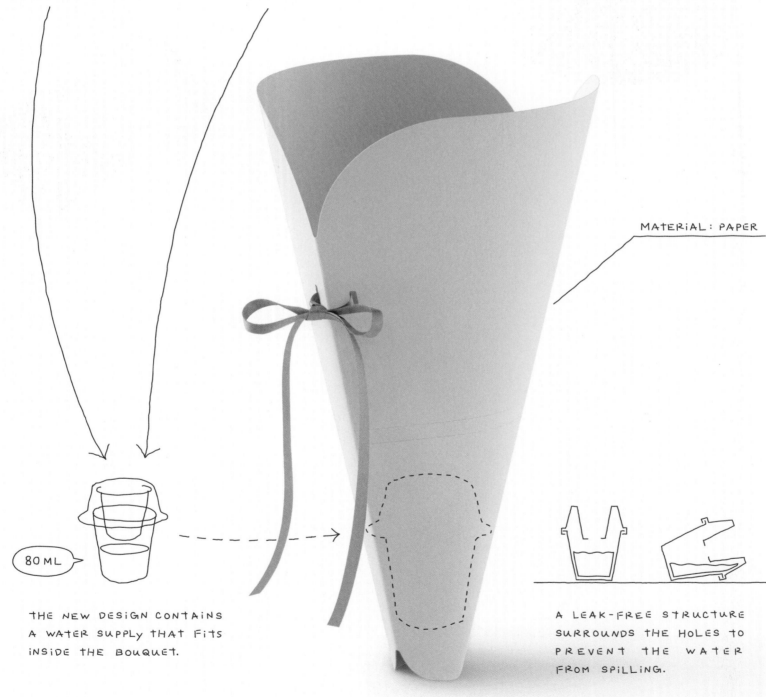

MATERIAL: PAPER

80 ML

THE NEW DESIGN CONTAINS A WATER SUPPLY THAT FITS INSIDE THE BOUQUET.

A LEAK-FREE STRUCTURE SURROUNDS THE HOLES TO PREVENT THE WATER FROM SPILLING.

SEPARATE

CUT ALONG LINE

26

BOUQUET

17

FLOWER VASE

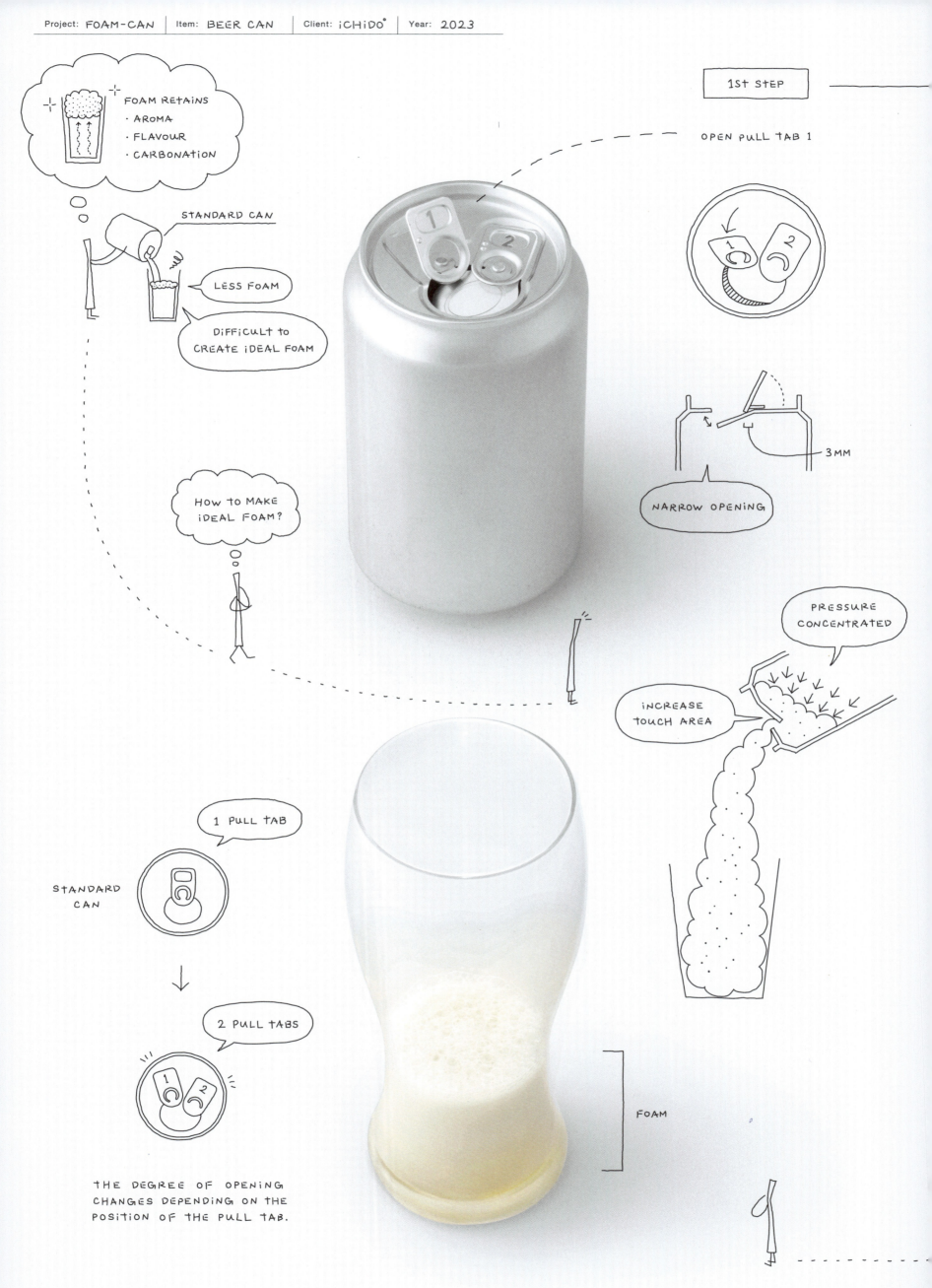

FOAM RETAINS
· AROMA
· FLAVOUR
· CARBONATION

STANDARD CAN

LESS FOAM

DIFFICULT to CREATE iDEAL FOAM

HOW TO MAKE iDEAL FOAM?

1 PULL TAB

STANDARD CAN

2 PULL TABS

THE DEGREE OF OPENING CHANGES DEPENDING ON THE POSITION OF THE PULL TAB.

1st STEP

OPEN PULL TAB 1

3MM

NARROW OPENING

PRESSURE CONCENTRATED

iNCREASE TOUCH AREA

FOAM

2ND STEP

OPEN PULL TAB 2

MATERIAL: ALUMINIUM

6 MM

WIDE OPENING

12

Ø 6.5

POUR THE REST OF THE LIQUID

③ FOAM

⑦ LIQUID

A GLASS WITH A LIQUID-TO-FOAM RATIO OF 7:3, THE SO-CALLED GOLDEN RATIO CAN NOW BE EASILY ACHIEVED WITH CANNED BEER.